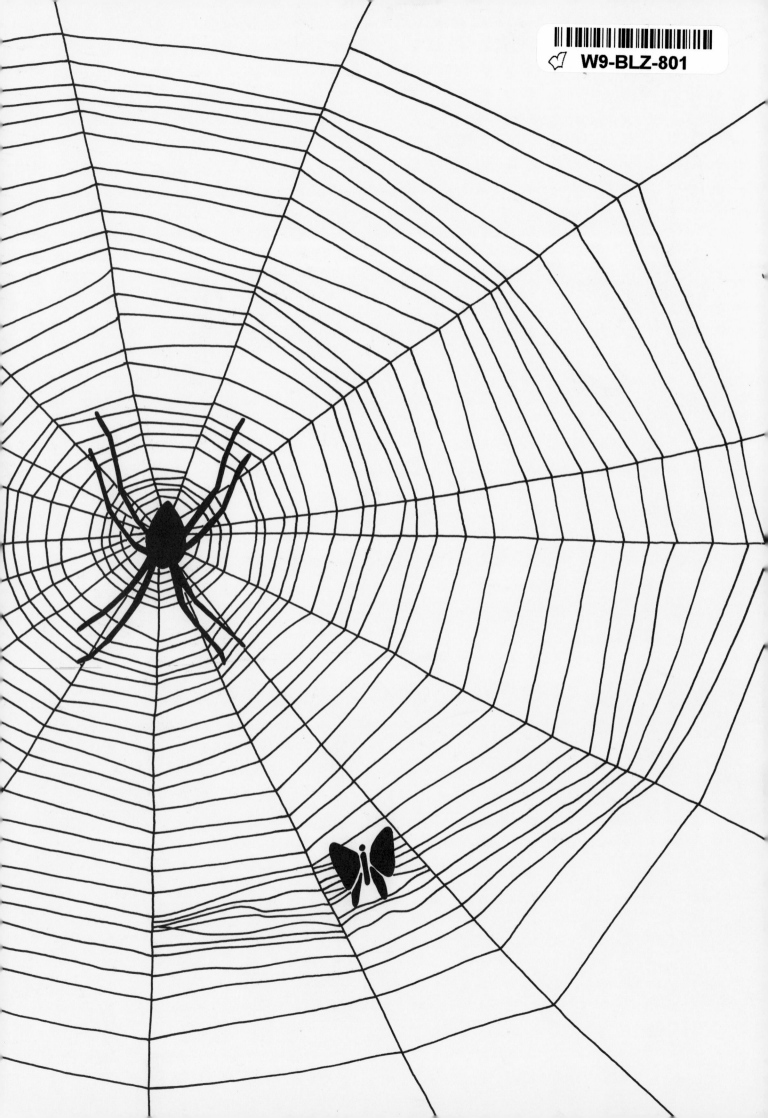

Insects & Spiders

TIME-LIFE
ALEXANDRIA, VIRGINIA

CONTENTS

4 Insect and Spider Nests

5 A Diversity of Defenses

6 The Complex Lives of Social Insects

1

Body Form and Function

Insects are among the oldest creatures on Earth. They evolved from other invertebrates—animals without backbones—more than 350 million years ago. Insects have spread over the entire planet, thriving in habitats ranging from desert to jungle, from hot spring to glacier. With more than a million species identified, insects are also the most successful at survival, making up about five-sixths of the animals on Earth. Insects belong to the arthropod phylum, along with classes that include spiders, crabs, pill bugs, and centipedes.

Starting life as eggs, insects either grow

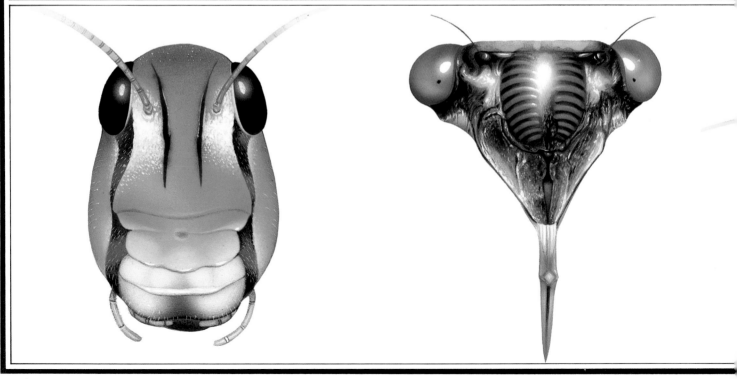

through larval and pupal stages, in which they look very different from the adults they will become; or they change from egg to nymph, a stage in which the young look similar to the adults and gradually develop wings as they grow. The typical insect body has three parts—head, thorax, and abdomen—with six legs and four wings attached to the thorax. Other arthropods, such as spiders, combine head and thorax in one segment and have eight legs but no wings. Centipedes and millipedes have many body segments, each with its own two (or four) legs.

These are just a few of the variations in the bodies of insects and their relatives—a population that is so diverse it boggles the mind. This book will explore the fascinating world of these creatures, starting with a look at how they evolved.

Even among flying insects, such as the cicada, ladybug, crane fly, and dragonfly *(above, from left)*, body structures vary enormously. Closeups of the heads *(below, from left)* of the grasshopper, cicada, praying mantis, and honeybee reveal their compound eyes.

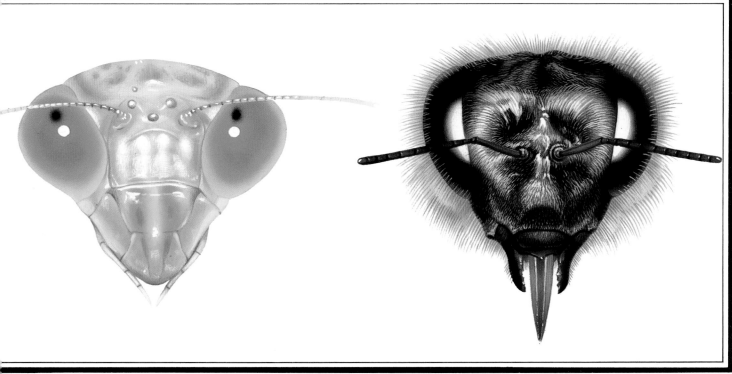

What Are Insects?

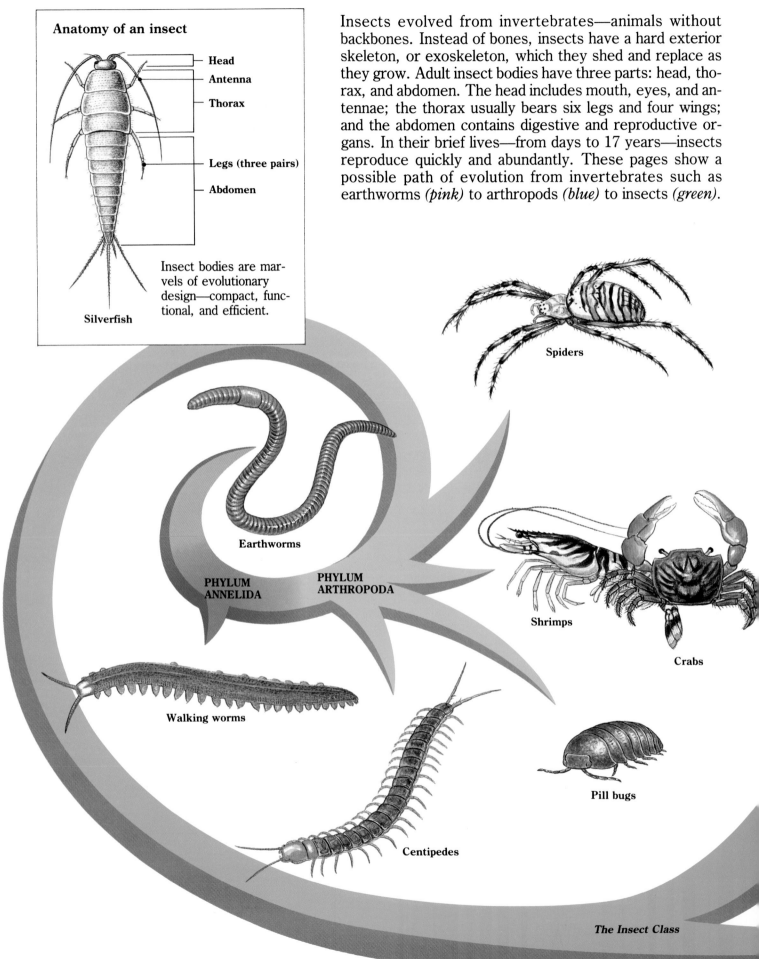

Silverfish

Head
Antenna
Thorax
Legs (three pairs)
Abdomen

Insect bodies are marvels of evolutionary design—compact, functional, and efficient.

Insects evolved from invertebrates—animals without backbones. Instead of bones, insects have a hard exterior skeleton, or exoskeleton, which they shed and replace as they grow. Adult insect bodies have three parts: head, thorax, and abdomen. The head includes mouth, eyes, and antennae; the thorax usually bears six legs and four wings; and the abdomen contains digestive and reproductive organs. In their brief lives—from days to 17 years—insects reproduce quickly and abundantly. These pages show a possible path of evolution from invertebrates such as earthworms *(pink)* to arthropods *(blue)* to insects *(green)*.

Spiders

Earthworms

PHYLUM ANNELIDA

PHYLUM ARTHROPODA

Shrimps

Crabs

Walking worms

Centipedes

Pill bugs

The Insect Class

6

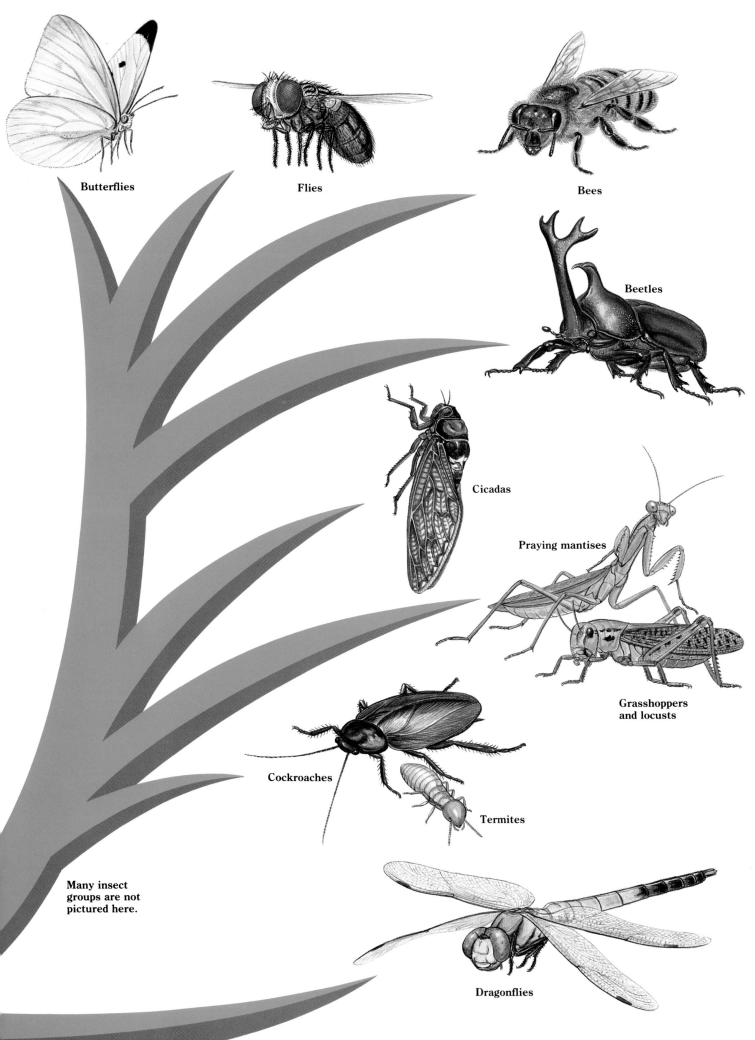

Butterflies

Flies

Bees

Beetles

Cicadas

Praying mantises

Grasshoppers
and locusts

Cockroaches

Termites

Many insect
groups are not
pictured here.

Dragonflies

Do Insects Have Hearts and Brains?

Insects have both a heart and a brain, but they function differently from a human being's. An insect's body fluids do not flow through a system of veins and arteries but circulate openly in the body cavity. Pumping these fluids is the dorsal vessel, located just under the insect's back. Built like a segmented tube, this vessel takes in the bloodlike body fluids and, through regular contractions of muscles attached to its outer walls *(below, bottom)*, pumps the fluids throughout the body.

The nervous system in the so-called lower insects, such as grasshoppers, dragonflies, and cockroaches, features ganglia, or nerve bundles, in each body segment as shown opposite at bottom. Two parallel lines of nerves connect the ganglia, and other nerves reach into each segment. The brain is at the tip of the head, and nerves connect it to the antennae, compound eyes, and mouth. Separate nerves in each body segment control muscle movement and breathing. Because of its segmented nervous system, an insect's body continues to move even if its head is cut off.

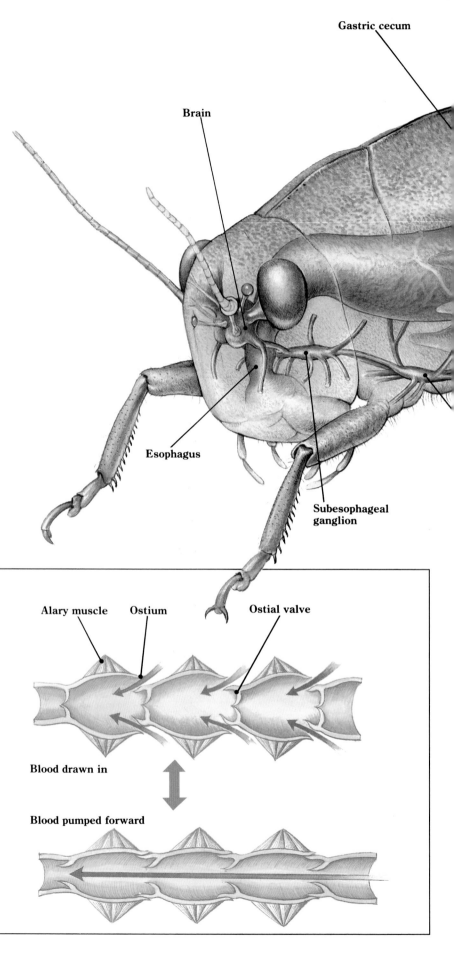

Gastric cecum

Brain

Esophagus

Subesophageal ganglion

How the dorsal vessel pumps

The dorsal blood vessel of an insect, consisting of the aorta and the heart, is a tube with as many as 12 chambers. On the sides of each chamber are opening valves called ostia. When the alary muscles outside the dorsal vessel contract, they widen the vessel, and body fluids flow in through each ostium *(right, top)*. When the muscles relax *(right, bottom)*, the ostial valves close, preventing backflow, and the vessel squeezes its contents, pumping the fluid toward the head. Most insects have a pulse of from 15 to 150 beats per minute, depending on their size and activity. A silkworm's heart *(right)* beats 50 to 60 times per minute. The pulsing of the dorsal vessel can actually be seen through the nearly transparent skin of certain caterpillars.

Alary muscle   Ostium   Ostial valve

Blood drawn in

Blood pumped forward

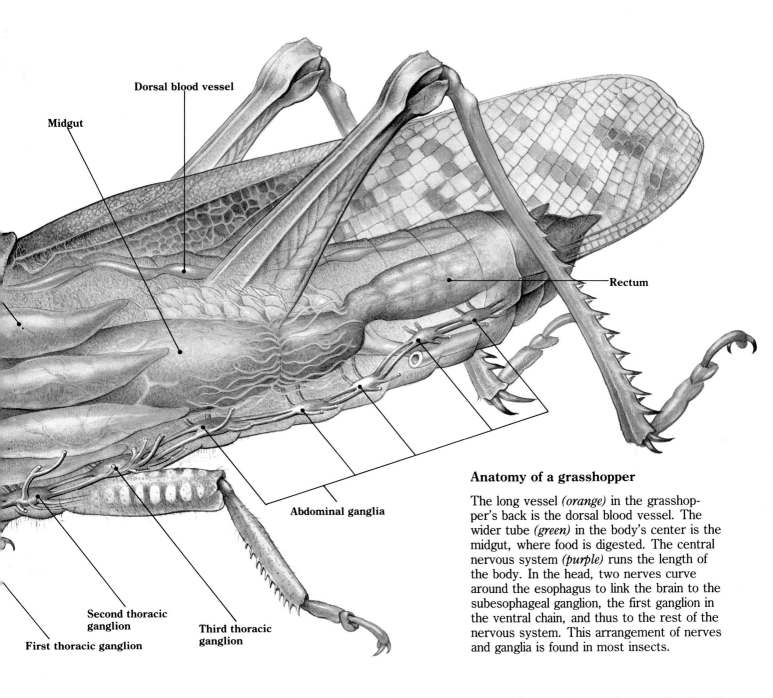

Dorsal blood vessel

Midgut

Rectum

Abdominal ganglia

Second thoracic ganglion

Third thoracic ganglion

First thoracic ganglion

Anatomy of a grasshopper

The long vessel *(orange)* in the grasshopper's back is the dorsal blood vessel. The wider tube *(green)* in the body's center is the midgut, where food is digested. The central nervous system *(purple)* runs the length of the body. In the head, two nerves curve around the esophagus to link the brain to the subesophageal ganglion, the first ganglion in the ventral chain, and thus to the rest of the nervous system. This arrangement of nerves and ganglia is found in most insects.

Nervous system

The grasshopper's central nervous system connects the brain and the nerve ganglia in each body segment. The head contains the brain and the subesophageal ganglion.

The grasshopper has three ganglia in its thorax and five in its abdomen. Small nerves originating in the ganglia control the activity of each segment—head, thorax, and abdomen. For example, the three ganglia in the thorax control the muscles that move the legs and the wings. Abdominal ganglia govern digestion and mating. The brain organizes the messages from the antennae and the compound eyes and coordinates overall body movement.

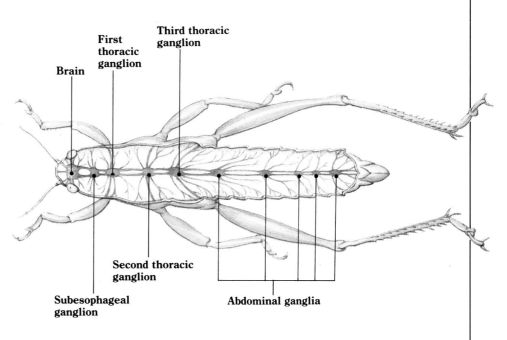

Brain

First thoracic ganglion

Third thoracic ganglion

Second thoracic ganglion

Subesophageal ganglion

Abdominal ganglia

How Do Insects Breathe?

Insects breathe by taking in oxygen and discharging carbon dioxide, just as other animals do. But insects have a system of tiny tubes called tracheae, distributed throughout the body, to deliver oxygen directly to the cells and organs. This system differs from mammals' pulmonary respiration, in which blood picks up oxygen in the lungs and carries it to the cells.

Air enters an insect's tracheae through tiny pores called spiracles and circulates through smaller tubes called tracheoles, which resemble capillaries. Body tissues take oxygen from the tracheoles and release carbon dioxide into them.

Spiracles are the tiny portholes and slits *(blue arrows)* along this beetle's abdomen.

Honeybee respiration. Air enters the bee's body through the spiracles and is distributed by the tracheal system.

Aquatic insects with gills

Insect nymphs living underwater obtain oxygen through gills in many shapes. Such internal or external tracheal gills occur in insects with a closed system that is lacking in functional spiracles. Oxygen from the water enters the bodies across the gill for delivery to the tracheoles. Dragonfly nymphs have rectal gills *(right, bottom);* mayfly and damselfly nymphs sport caudal gills at the end of their tails *(right, top).*

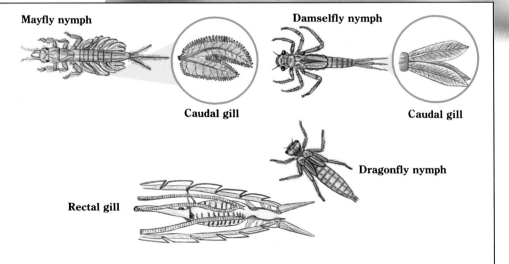

Mayfly nymph

Damselfly nymph

Caudal gill

Caudal gill

Dragonfly nymph

Rectal gill

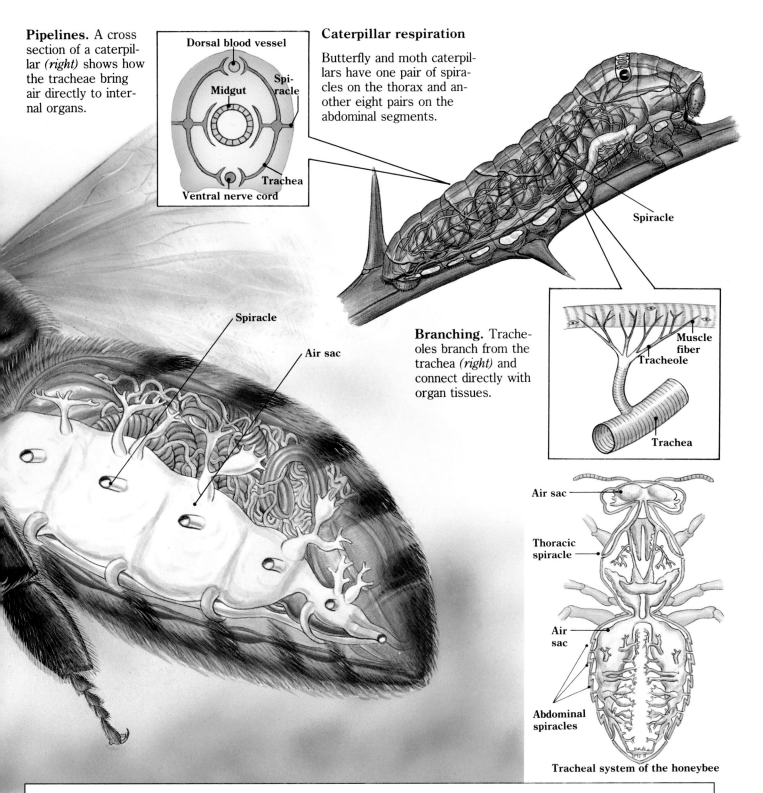

Pipelines. A cross section of a caterpillar *(right)* shows how the tracheae bring air directly to internal organs.

Dorsal blood vessel

Midgut

Spiracle

Trachea

Ventral nerve cord

Caterpillar respiration

Butterfly and moth caterpillars have one pair of spiracles on the thorax and another eight pairs on the abdominal segments.

Spiracle

Branching. Tracheoles branch from the trachea *(right)* and connect directly with organ tissues.

Muscle fiber

Tracheole

Trachea

Spiracle

Air sac

Air sac

Thoracic spiracle

Air sac

Abdominal spiracles

Tracheal system of the honeybee

An insect "Aqua-Lung"

Some adult aquatic insects such as the water beetle at right have extra-tracheal air stores under their wings to use underwater. When oxygen in the stored air is depleted by respiration, the beetle forms an air bubble at the end of its abdomen. The air in this "physical gill" is refreshed as carbon dioxide goes into the water and oxygen from the water enters the bubble. This "gill" permits the beetle to stay submerged.

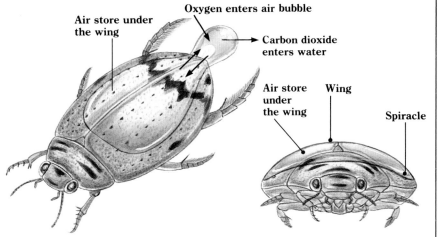

Air store under the wing

Oxygen enters air bubble

Carbon dioxide enters water

Air store under the wing

Wing

Spiracle

How Can a Thousand-Legger Walk?

Centipedes and millipedes—"hundred-leggers" and "thousand-leggers"—account for most of the species in the arthropod class known as Myriapoda—"many-footed." Unlike their insect cousins, myriapods have many legs but no wings. They cannot close their spiracles to conserve moisture and so risk drying out in sunlight. To stay comfortable, they live in dark, humid places and are most active at night.

With between nine and 200 pairs of legs, centipedes and millipedes have unique methods of walking. In general, their legs move in regular waves *(opposite),* which start at the front and move to the rear.

Centipede or millipede?

Centipedes and millipedes differ in several important ways. Centipedes have one pair of legs attached to each body segment *(right, top),* while millipedes have two pairs of legs for each segment *(right, bottom).* Centipedes are hunters, preying on other animals such as earthworms and even small vertebrates, including toads and mice. They dispatch their prey by paralyzing them with their poisonous jaws, then devour them. Most millipedes are vegetarians and play an important role in soil formation by breaking down rotting leaves.

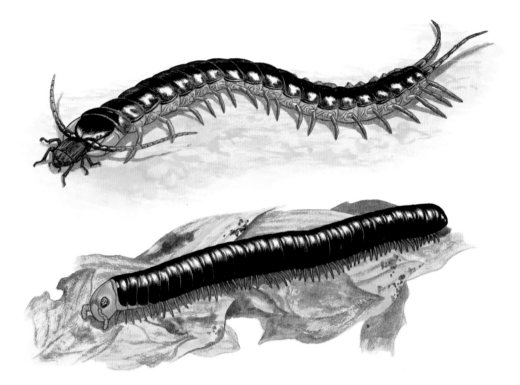

● How six-legged insects walk

Six-legged insects, such as the ground beetles below, walk by moving three legs at a time, two on one side and one on the other. The three stationary legs form a stable tripod while the other three move forward in a similar triangular pattern. In each pair of legs, when one is touching the ground, the other is moving. The stability provided by this repeated tripod pattern lets insects move fast without tripping or tipping over.

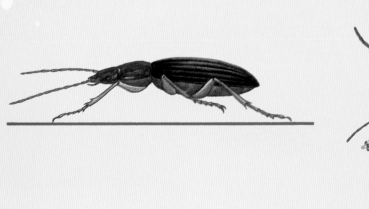

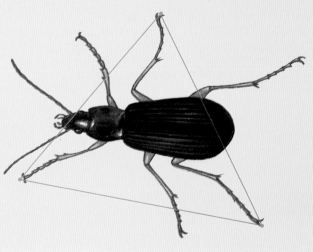

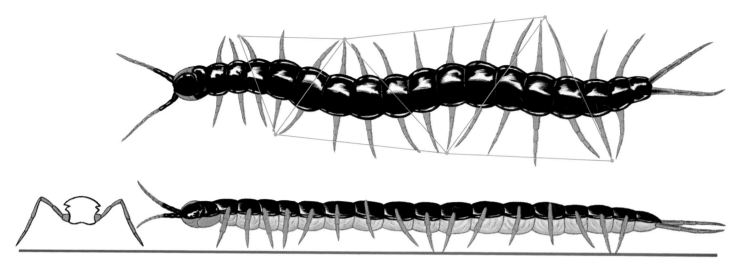

How a centipede walks

Seen from above, some of a walking centipede's legs are close together, while others are spread apart. Lines drawn between points where the legs touch the ground form triangles, showing that the centipede uses the same basic tripod gait that six-legged insects use. Only the legs at the points of the triangles touch the ground at any given moment, while the other legs are raised and in motion. To form these triangles, a centipede swings its body from side to side. The body stays low to the ground even in motion, for a low center of gravity and great stability.

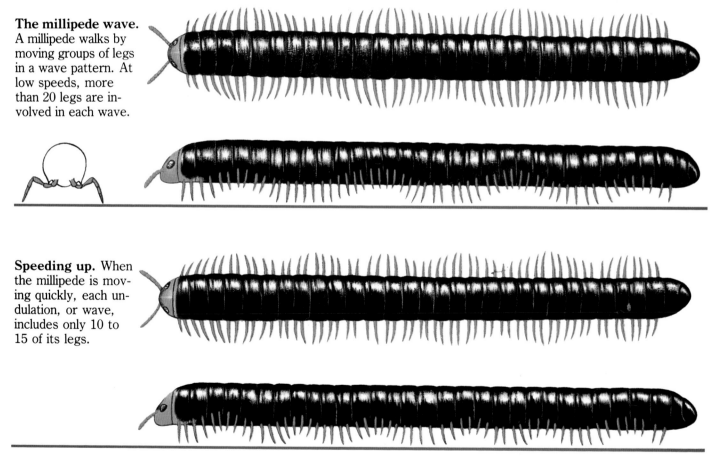

The millipede wave. A millipede walks by moving groups of legs in a wave pattern. At low speeds, more than 20 legs are involved in each wave.

Speeding up. When the millipede is moving quickly, each undulation, or wave, includes only 10 to 15 of its legs.

Millipedes in motion

Millipedes, unlike six-legged insects and centipedes, do not use a tripod walking pattern. Instead, they move both legs in each pair in unison—similar to the oars in a rowboat. They lift as many as 50 legs at a time in a regular wavelike undulation, slowly pushing themselves forward. Another difference is that while the centipede's legs, attached midway up its flattened body, give it great stability, the millipede's legs are attached to the underside of its round, rather rigid body. This body shape and gait make the millipede slower and less stable than the centipede. But because it is a scavenger rather than a hunter, the millipede does not really need speed. In fact, it often uses the strength of its legs for burrowing in search of food. For protection, it relies on a secretion that has a strong and unpleasant scent, which encourages potential predators to look elsewhere for a meal.

How Do Insects Fly?

Many insects are too heavy to glide; they fly by flapping their wings vigorously. Most species have two pairs of wings, but in many species these are joined and work together, as in the butterfly. Flies and mosquitoes flap only the front pair of wings, using the rear pair—reduced to small knobbed structures—as stabilizers. Dragonflies, by contrast, have two pairs of long, narrow wings that flap alternately, giving them exceptional agility.

Dragonfly. The pairs of wings beat alternately: As the front wings go up, the rear ones go down.

Cicada. The cicada has two pairs of wings but a heavy body; it can fly fast but not for a very long time.

Insect aviators

The table at right compares the speeds of insects in flight, arranged from top to bottom in order of speed. Fast fliers have less wing area and greater body weight, which helps them overcome air resistance. The fastest flier is the hawk moth, which is built for speed with a narrow body and powerful forewings. The dragonfly's four wings operate independently and can be slanted for greater lift and power. During fast flight, the dragonfly folds its legs under its body to reduce drag. Very small insects, hampered by air resistance because of their small weight and size, find it easier to float on the air currents rather than fly.

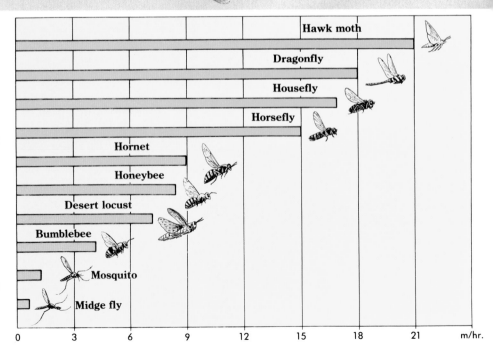

Hawk moth

Dragonfly

Housefly

Horsefly

Hornet

Honeybee

Desert locust

Bumblebee

Mosquito

Midge fly

0   3   6   9   12   15   18   21   m/hr.

Butterfly. The butterfly's wings are short but wide, and large for its body size. Butterflies can flap their wings slowly or glide, enabling some species to migrate far.

Honeybee. The bee's wings are small for its body but beat 200 times per second, letting the bee fly far or hover in one spot.

Beetle. The long-horned beetle's flapping rear wings provide power in flight, while its fixed forewings add lift.

Mosquito. A mosquito flaps its long front wings up to 600 times per second, creating a hum. The modified rear wings add stability.

Insect wings and their muscles

Insect wings are not appendages, like legs; they are thin outgrowths of the exoskeleton, evolved for flight. In different species, the wings are powered through direct or indirect muscle structure. In a dragonfly *(right, top),* the muscles are attached directly to the wing bases, which turn on a fulcrum between the muscles. Contractions of outer muscles lower the wings; contractions of inner muscles raise them.

In the bee *(right, bottom),* the fulcrums are where the wings enter the body, and the wing bases are moved when muscles change the shape of the body. Wings go up when two vertical muscles in the trunk contract *(near right, bottom, pink).* Wings go down with contraction of a lengthwise muscle *(far right, bottom, pink).* With either type of wing structure, the muscles are elastic and flap the wings at a fixed rate.

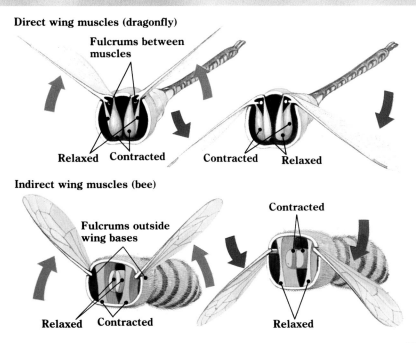

Direct wing muscles (dragonfly)

Fulcrums between muscles

Relaxed Contracted

Contracted Relaxed

Indirect wing muscles (bee)

Fulcrums outside wing bases

Contracted

Relaxed Contracted

Relaxed

What Makes Fleas Jump So High?

Fleas are famous for their ability to jump. These wingless, bloodsucking parasites, about ⅟₂₅ of an inch long, have been seen to jump more than a foot. To perform an equivalent feat, a 4-foot-tall child would have to jump farther than the length of four football fields. There are more than 1,500 species of fleas, most of them living on only one or two species of mammals or birds as their host. They jump onto likely hosts passing by, even birds in flight.

Fleas are descended from winged insects but lost the wings, probably so as to burrow more easily through fur and feathers to the flesh and blood of their hosts. The flea's small, narrow body has a rounded thorax and enlarged, heavily muscled hind legs. Its great jumping ability arises from a structure called the pleural (for "rib") arch, which is made of a rubberlike protein called resilin. A flea preparing to jump compresses its pleural arch *(below, second picture),* storing the muscles' energy there. When the pleural arch is released, as much as 97 percent of the energy stored in it is suddenly unleashed, propelling the flea through the air in a mighty leap.

■ **How a flea jumps**

A flea walks on all six of its legs, much like any other insect.

Preparing to jump *(below),* a flea crouches, bending its hind legs and compressing the pleural arch.

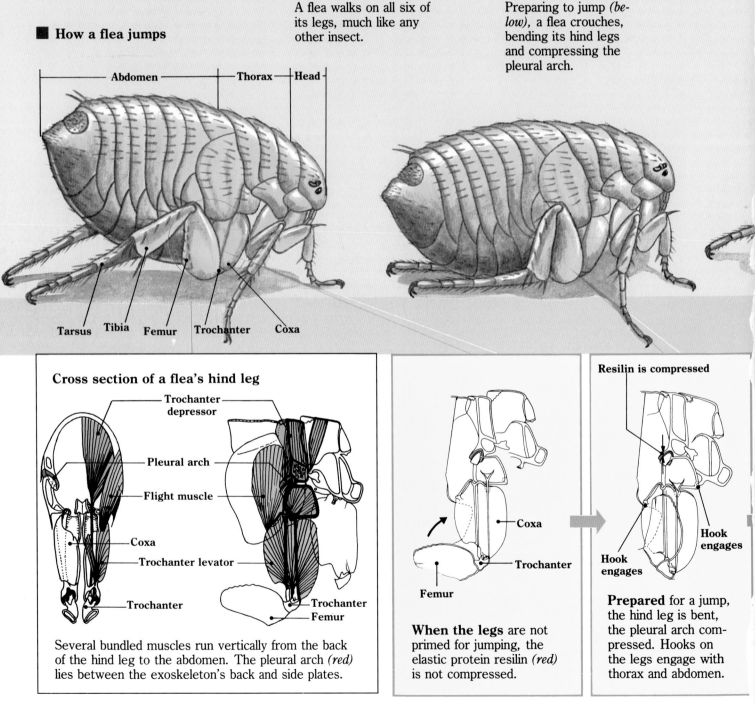

Abdomen — Thorax — Head

Tarsus Tibia Femur Trochanter Coxa

Cross section of a flea's hind leg

Trochanter depressor

Pleural arch

Flight muscle

Coxa

Trochanter levator

Trochanter

Trochanter
Femur

Several bundled muscles run vertically from the back of the hind leg to the abdomen. The pleural arch *(red)* lies between the exoskeleton's back and side plates.

Coxa

Trochanter

Femur

When the legs are not primed for jumping, the elastic protein resilin *(red)* is not compressed.

Resilin is compressed

Hook
engages

Hook
engages

Hook
engages

Prepared for a jump, the hind leg is bent, the pleural arch compressed. Hooks on the legs engage with thorax and abdomen.

The tips of the hind legs leave the surface and the flea is airborne, for as long as ¹⁄₁₀ of a second.

As the pleural arch is released, its energy snaps the hind leg straight, lifting the flea's body.

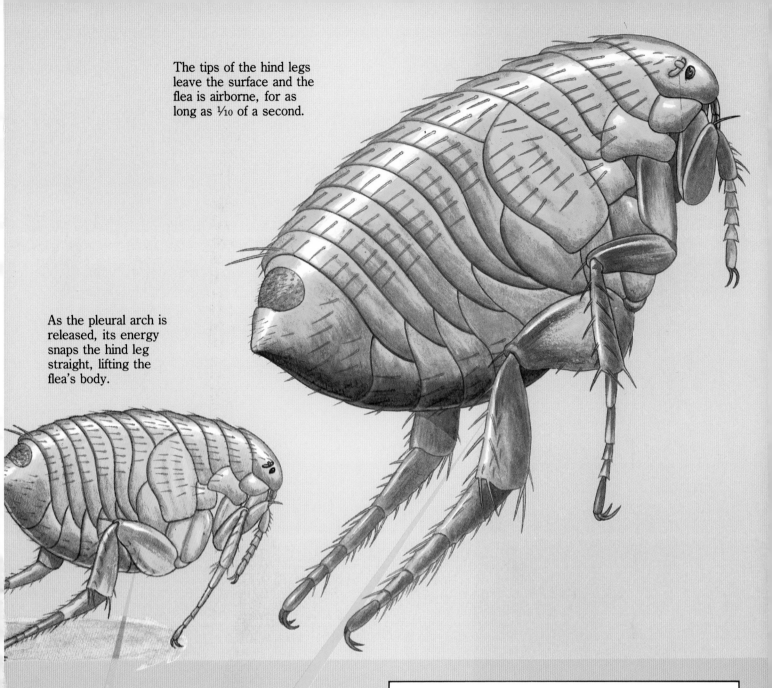

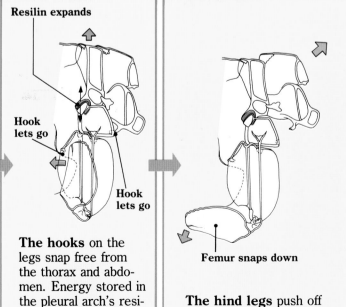

Resilin expands

Hook lets go

Hook lets go

The hooks on the legs snap free from the thorax and abdomen. Energy stored in the pleural arch's resilin is released.

Femur snaps down

The hind legs push off and the flea jumps.

The perfect host

Different types of fleas prefer particular hosts and have ingenious ways of finding them. Most fleas jump in response to exhaled carbon dioxide. But mouse fleas recognize the mouse's odor. Fleas that live on martins hibernate in the birds' abandoned nests, then jump in response to the heat, air currents, and shadows of the returning birds' flapping wings in the spring. Rabbit fleas are sensitive to hormones in their hosts' bloodstreams and mate only when the rabbits do.

In an experiment, cat fleas jumped from the sand when carbon dioxide entered the flask.

Can Insects Walk on Water?

A variety of insects spend their lives atop the very surface of water in lakes, streams, and ponds, or even in the ocean. The most familiar of these insects is the long-legged water strider *(below)*, but others such as the water measurer and the whirligig beetle are also at home on the water's surface.

All of these insects take advantage of a property of liquids known as surface tension. The water's surface forms a thin and elastic film, or membrane, on which lightweight insects can stand and walk, making shallow dimplelike depressions in the film. Water striders have evolved specialized anatomical structures that let them move quickly and efficiently over the water's surface. Most water-walking insects have oil glands at the ends of their legs to keep them from getting waterlogged.

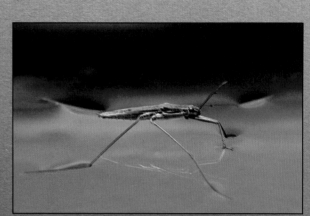

Striders. The widely spread legs of the water strider distribute its weight over a large surface.

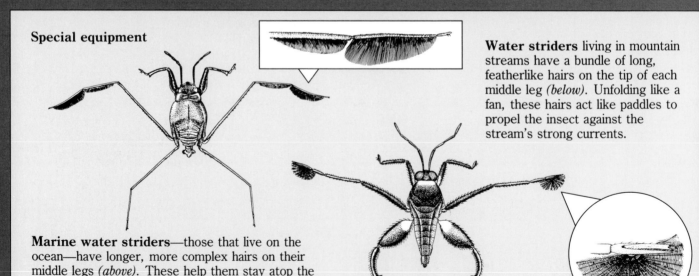

Special equipment

Water striders living in mountain streams have a bundle of long, featherlike hairs on the tip of each middle leg *(below)*. Unfolding like a fan, these hairs act like paddles to propel the insect against the stream's strong currents.

Marine water striders—those that live on the ocean—have longer, more complex hairs on their middle legs *(above)*. These help them stay atop the water and help them push against the water's surface as they stride across it.

Row, row, row your boat. For maximum power, the water strider *Microvelia douglasi* paddles simultaneously with both the left and right middle legs, pushing off against the dimples it makes in the surface film. When gliding over the surface *(below)*, it stands on all six legs, steering with its hind legs.

Grabbers. For greater traction, water striders have tiny claws, set back from the tips of the feet so as not to break the water's film.

Walking on water

Water striders and their relatives have two ways of moving over the water's surface. Some stand on their front and back legs and kick backward with the middle legs, to push the body forward. Others, like the water measurer of the family Hydrometridae *(left)*, walk on water with the same gait used by land insects. The insect forms a stable tripod of two legs on one side and one on the other side *(black legs at left, top)*, while the other three legs *(blue, left, second from top)* move ahead. For the next step, the pattern is reversed.

How Do Flies Walk on the Ceiling?

Houseflies and other insects can often be seen walking upside down on the ceiling or up a smooth windowpane of glass, apparently defying gravity. How do they do it? The secret lies in special structures of their legs.

Between the claws at the tip of each leg, flies have a pair of adhesive pads. Each pad is shaped like a suction cup and has on it hundreds of extremely fine hairs. Glands in the pads release an oily secretion through the hairs, which helps the fly to stick to whatever surface it stands on.

Flies are not the only insects that are built this way. Ladybugs, leaf beetles, honeybees, cabbage butterflies, and cockroaches have similarly specialized feet, and they too can walk on glass or across ceilings.

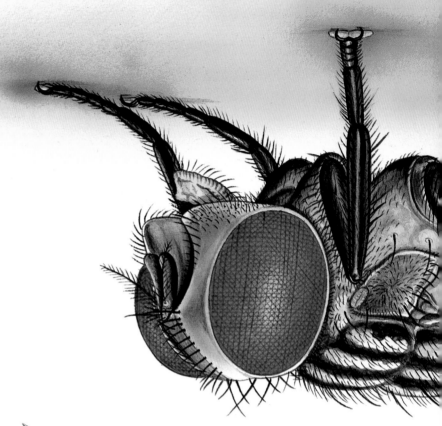

The mighty grip of the ladybug

The ladybug can walk on ceilings or on vertical surfaces, just like a fly. On the inner side of the tips of its first and second legs *(far right)*, the ladybug has about 800 ultrafine hairs, growing uniformly in the same direction. Each hair ends in a spoon-shaped tip.

Like the fly, the ladybug secretes a sticky, oily substance—probably from these hairs—which enables it to walk upside down. Traces of these secretions can be seen in the ladybug's footprints on laboratory slides. In one experiment *(near right)*, weights are attached to the ladybug, and it walks upside down on a glass microscope slide. An adult ladybug weighs only about .1 ounce, yet it can support some five times its own weight without losing its grip on the glass.

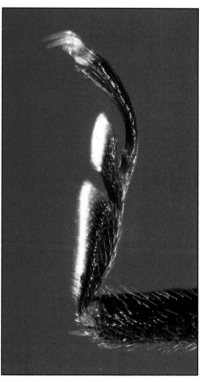

Gripping tip of ladybug's leg

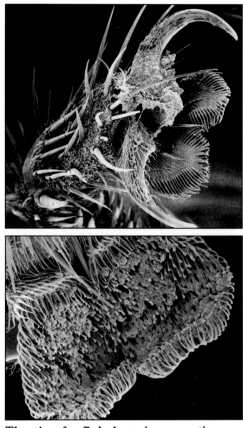

The tip of a fly's leg—here greatly magnified under a scanning electron microscope—includes claws and pads *(above, top)*. On each pad *(above, bottom)* are many fine hairs. Oil that is secreted from glands in the pad helps the fly stick to sheer surfaces and support about twice its own weight.

Skywalkers and ground dwellers

Insects that can walk on ceilings and vertical glass surfaces are generally small and lightweight. They all have special leg adaptations, such as the fly's pads and the fine hairs on the ladybug's legs. In nature, these adaptations help the insects perch on flowers and leaves, where they can easily catch prey.

Other insects, such as those shown at right, bottom, cannot cling to these surfaces because they lack the specialized leg structures for this purpose. These insects are usually larger and heavier, and live on the ground or on tree trunks. The structure of an insect's legs is closely related to the nature of its habitat. Over time, each insect species has evolved adaptations useful for survival in a certain habitat.

Insects that cling and their foot structures

Honeybee   Cabbage butterfly   Cockroach

Insects that do not cling and their foot structures

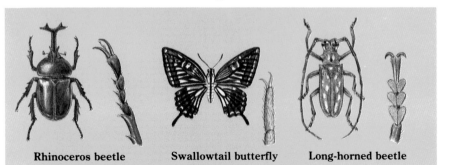

Rhinoceros beetle   Swallowtail butterfly   Long-horned beetle

How Can Insects See?

Besides their large compound eyes, insects have another organ that is sensitive to light. Called the ocellus, this organ has an eyelike structure but does not sense true images. Rather, the ocelli respond to changes in light intensity, by stimulating the insect to increase or decrease its activity.

During the larval stage of development, the ocelli in most insects are lateral—that is, located on the sides of the head. In most adult insects, the ocelli are dorsal—on the top or back of the head.

■ The ocelli and insect activity

The stimulation of light falling on the ocelli makes walking insects walk faster and flying insects fly faster.

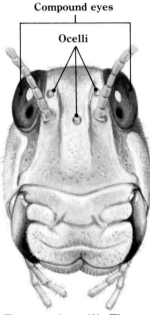

Eyes and ocelli. The cicada has three ocelli between its eyes.

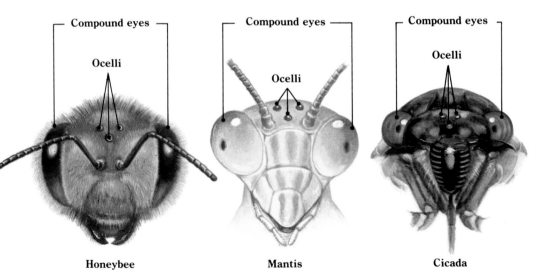

Blackout. If all of the ocelli are covered, the insect will not move toward a bright light.

Ocellus varieties

The majority of adult insects have three ocelli, arranged in a triangular pattern on the forehead. The center ocellus is believed to be two fused primitive ocelli; in structure it is similar to the eyes of dragonflies and honeybees. The ocelli develop when the wings do, and most wingless insects have no ocelli. Nocturnal moths also lack this light-sensitive organ. The structure of the ocelli varies greatly from species to species.

Honeybee

Mantis

Cicada

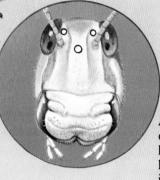

All systems go. With all ocelli open to the light, a locust walks toward the light at a speed of 1½ inches per second.

Slowdown. A locust with its center ocellus covered walks slower than normal, at an inch per second.

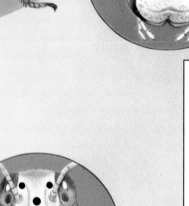

Ocellus structure

The ocellus has tens to hundreds of vision cells behind a corneal lens and the corneagen layer of transparent skin cells. Among the vision cells are rhabdoms, containing photoreactive pigments that absorb light. Pigmented areas outside the vision cells may also affect light perception. The ocelli perceive even weak light but cannot form images.

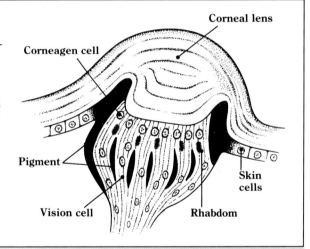

Corneal lens

Corneagen cell

Pigment

Vision cell

Skin cells

Rhabdom

Effects of the ocelli

The ocelli influence not only an insect's flying and walking speed but also its general level of activity. Compared with normal honeybees, a bee with its ocelli covered *(bottom right)* begins gathering food later in the morning (when sunlight is brighter) and returns to the hive earlier in the evening. A housefly with its ocelli darkened *(far right)* will not move at all, even in daylight. Other flies with their ocelli obscured react only slowly to changes in light intensity.

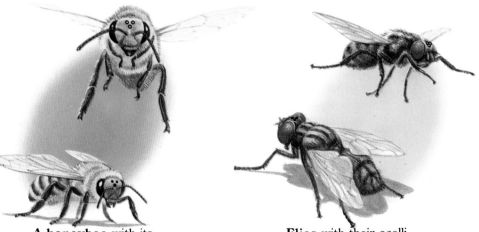

A honeybee with its ocelli covered starts work later in the day and quits earlier than normal.

Flies with their ocelli blackened remain motionless during the day.

What Can Insects Hear?

Bats search for their insect prey with sonar. As they fly, they emit sounds too high pitched for humans to hear and steer by the echoes. Research has shown that some insects—including nocturnal moths, black mayflies, crickets, and a type of mantis—hear these sounds and can evade the bats. In some moths, males also make ultrasonic sounds to attract mates.

A moth's ears

Certain moths detect sounds with two tympanic organs on the sides of the body. Named for a drum, or tympanum, which it resembles, the tympanic organ *(below)* is a membrane stretched drumlike over nerves in a pocket.

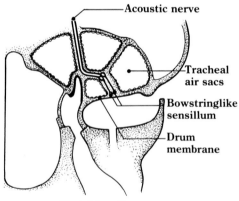

Noctuid moth ear

Hairs for hearing. Some moth species detect sounds by means of sensory hairs *(below)* together with air sacs in the palpi. Bats' ultrasonic waves make the hairs vibrate.

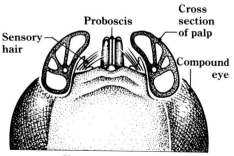

Hawk moth ear

Sensing enemy location

A moth's left and right tympanic organs hear independently. That is, signals are not equally strong on the two sides. The moth can identify where a bat's cries come from by the intensity of sound on one side or the other *(near right)*. A bat approaching from above *(far right)* sounds louder to the moth when its own wings are up.

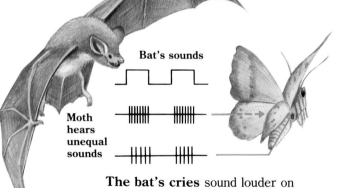

The bat's cries sound louder on the moth's left side, which is closer to the bat.

Evasive actions. Tiger moths, hawk moths, and others that can detect a bat's ultrasonic waves use several escape maneuvers. Moths below the transmitter power-dive or drop by folding their wings; those on a level with the transmitter fly off in an irregular pattern, heading away from the strongest sound waves.

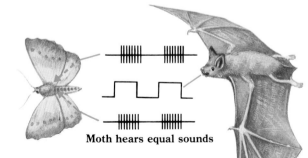

Moth hears equal sounds

When incoming sounds are equal in both tympanic organs, the moth knows that the bat is directly behind it.

If the bat's sounds are fainter when the moth's wings are down, the moth realizes that the bat is approaching from above.

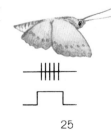

Moth hears muffled sounds

What Are Antennae Used For?

Although they don't look like noses, an insect's antennae serve mainly to detect odors. Flies and mosquitoes, for example, smell their food with their antennae. Many female insects, such as butterflies, use their antennae to check for competing insects' eggs on the plants where they intend to lay their eggs. Females and males of many families, including honeybees, long-horned beetles, and moths, use their antennae to detect the pheromones—odor-carrying molecules—that are released by potential mates. Their antennae also tell them which of their companions have already mated. Cockroaches find water or each other by detecting scents with their antennae.

Antennae have several other uses, too. Honeybees and ants touch antennae to distinguish between nest mates and intruders and to spread news about food sources and danger. Mosquitoes' antennae can also detect sound.

1

2

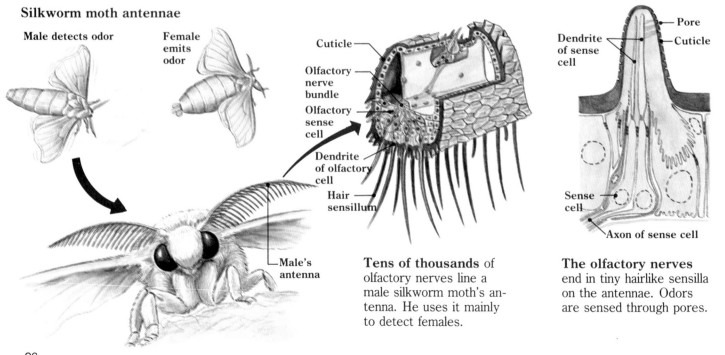

Silkworm moth antennae

Male detects odor

Female emits odor

Male's antenna

Cuticle

Olfactory nerve bundle

Olfactory sense cell

Dendrite of olfactory cell

Hair sensillum

Pore

Dendrite of sense cell

Cuticle

Sense cell

Axon of sense cell

Tens of thousands of olfactory nerves line a male silkworm moth's antenna. He uses it mainly to detect females.

The olfactory nerves end in tiny hairlike sensilla on the antennae. Odors are sensed through pores.

Chafer fans

Scarab beetles, like the cockchafer above, sport multibranched antenna blades that spread widely apart during flight to determine wind direction and detect any smells that would lead them to a food source. On the ground the beetle closes its antenna into a thin branch.

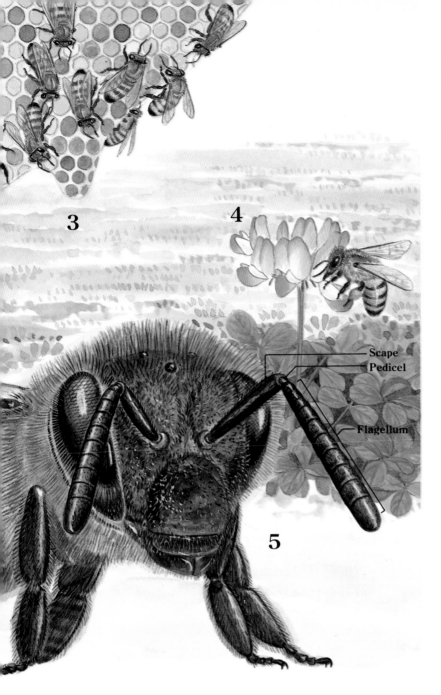

Scape
Pedicel

Flagellum

3

4

5

1. Identity check. Worker bees often touch antennae, communicating by smell.

2. Food alert. A bee dances to announce a new source of nectar to nest mates and passes along a sample of the nectar.

3. Measurement. Honeybees use their antennae to measure wall thicknesses as they build the hexagonal cells of their nests.

4. Flower check. Honeybees gather nectar from flowers as a carbohydrate source and pollen as a protein source to raise the young.

5. Anatomy. Bee antennae are two-part jointed stalks, containing several types of sensilla, or sensory organs.

Pheromones and mating

The male silkworm moth's antenna is specially equipped to detect the females' pheromones. When a female is ready to mate, she secretes a liquid pheromone called bombykol from a gland at the end of her abdomen. The odor stimulates the male moth to mate with her. Bombykol was the first pheromone to be chemically analyzed by scientists. The male's antennae can spot extremely tiny amounts of this pheromone—perhaps even a single molecule—carried on the breeze. Once the moth senses this odor, he flaps his wings faster and follows the pheromone trail to the female moth who is emitting it.

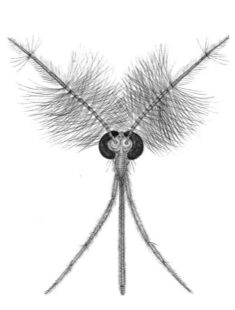

A mosquito's Johnston's organ

Fine hairs on a male mosquito's antennae *(left)* sense air currents and sounds. Around the base of each antenna is the Johnston's organ *(above),* which alerts the males to the specific sound made by the wings of a female of his own species.

How Do Insects Make Sounds?

On a warm summer night, backyards can erupt in a virtual symphony of insect sounds. These sounds are not mere noise. They are the male insects' way of attracting potential female mates and warning off rivals and predators.

Crickets make sounds by rubbing the ridged edges of their wing covers together *(below)*. Grasshoppers rub ridges on their hind legs against other ridges on their abdomens or wing covers. A grasshopper seeking a mate may make

his sound as often as 50 million times in a summer. Both crickets and grasshoppers rub their wings faster in warmer weather.

The male cicada *(opposite)* has a sound organ on his abdomen, along with a hollow resonating chamber that amplifies the sound. The long-horned beetle uses a special sound organ located at the joint between the thorax and abdomen; with it, he makes loud noises intended to warn off potential enemies.

■ **The cricket's sound organ**

Raising his wings, the male cricket rubs the ridged structures on each wing together to make sounds.

Ears. Crickets hear with a drumlike membrane in each foreleg.

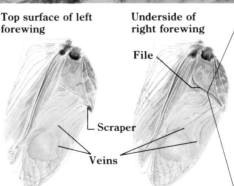

Song. A cricket runs one wing's file over the other's scraper.

Sound resonates in this space

Scraper — File

The instrument. When the right wing *(right)* is folded over the left *(left)*, the file meets the scraper.

Top surface of left forewing

Underside of right forewing

File

Scraper

Veins

Closeup. Magnified 200 times, the surface of the file shows its numerous even ridges.

28

The male cicada's sound organ

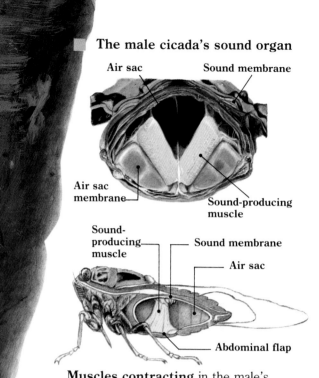

Air sac   Sound membrane

Air sac membrane

Sound-producing muscle

Sound-producing muscle   Sound membrane

Air sac

Abdominal flap

Muscles contracting in the male's sound organ vibrate the air sac, and the hollow abdomen resonates.

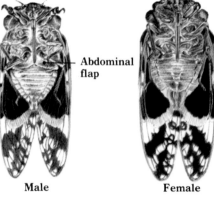

Abdominal flap

Male   **Female**

The male *(left)* has a sound organ on the upper abdomen, covered by a large abdominal flap.

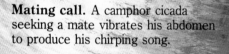

Mating call. A camphor cicada seeking a mate vibrates his abdomen to produce his chirping song.

Long-horned beetle threats

On meeting an enemy, the long-horned beetle produces a loud, threatening sound with a sound organ between his thorax and abdomen. He makes this sound by rasping the thorax across the ridges of the sound organ. Vigorous vibration creates a sound loud enough to warn off potential predators. This beetle also makes other, quieter sounds by rubbing together other joints of its body.

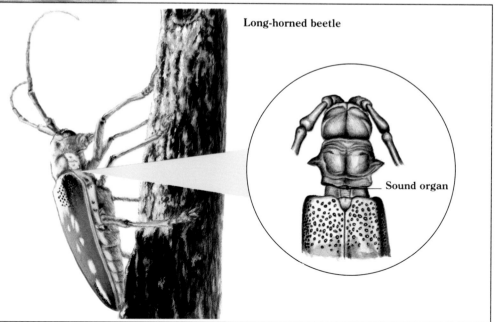

Long-horned beetle

Sound organ

What Colors a Butterfly's Wings?

Mosaic. Greatly magnified, the wing of the orange-tipped butterfly looks like a grid. Each cell holds grains of pigment.

Scales. Magnification of the tiger swallowtail's wing shows a complex pattern of tiny scales.

Closeup. Greater magnification *(right)* reveals a honeycomb structure, which holds the scale's grains of pigment.

Network. Magnified further *(above)*, each scale has ribs.

The glittering morpho

The South American morpho, with shimmering, iridescent blue wings, is one of the most beautiful of butterflies. Yet when the scales on its wings are examined under a microscope, they appear colorless. The morpho's secret lies in the comblike structure of its scales, which act as prisms to reflect light.

Depending on the angle of the light, the scales either absorb the light and look colorless, or reflect it and produce the morpho's distinctive blue coloring, which can be seen for nearly a mile. As its wings flap and the light angle changes, the morpho's blue color is sometimes visible and sometimes not.

The South American morpho's color depends on the angle of the light.

Comblike structures in the morpho's scales act like prisms to reflect light.

The distinctive colors on the wings of butterflies and moths arise from intricate patterns of tiny scales. The red or yellow in a wing comes from tiny grains of pigment on the scales. Blue and green, however, are produced not by pigments but by scale surfaces shaped to reflect light—that is, to bounce it off the wing at an angle. Reflection and pigments can both occur on the same wing, creating a variety of patterns and color combinations. The black and white closeup photographs below are made by scanning electron microscopes, which do not show color.

Emblem. The giant purple butterfly of the nymphalid family is the official butterfly of Japan.

Two-toned. The gossamer-winged hairstreak butterfly has a hairlike tail.

Icy. *Parnassus glacialis,* a primitive swallowtail, has hairlike scales where the wings appear transparent.

How does color help an insect?

The wings of butterflies and moths are pleasant to look at, but the colors also serve vital functions. In some species they help attract mates, and in some they save the insect from being eaten—but not always by helping it to hide.

The brilliant reds and yellows of some butterfly wings serve as a warning: "I am not good to eat!" Monarch butterfly caterpillars feed on milkweed, which contains a poison that does not harm the butterfly but makes birds throw up. After eating one of these brightly colored insects, a bird quickly learns not to catch another, even when they are plentiful.

Wing with scales removed

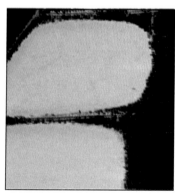

Colored membrane. The translucent blue areas *(above)* on the wings of the blue-striped swallowtail *(left)* bear no scales. Their color lies in pigment in the wing membrane.

Is It a Moth or a Butterfly?

Moths and butterflies are more alike than different and can be hard to classify. Butterflies, as a rule, fly by day, are brightly colored, perch with folded wings, and have thin, clubbed antennae. Moths have feathery or thickened antennae, dull colors, and wide bodies. They perch with open wings and fly at night. But many species break these rules.

The smoky moth *(above)* of the zygaenid family also flies in daylight.

The *Kaniska canace (right)* butterfly rests with its wings open.

The **typical** cabbage butterfly has a slim abdomen and perches with closed wings.

The **hummingbird** moth *(above)* flies by day, feeding on nectar like hummingbirds.

The **swallowtail** butterfly *(above)* displays its colors with its wings wide open.

Rules and exceptions

Most butterfly antennae are simple stalks, slightly thickened, or clubbed, at the tip *(top, near right)*. Most moths have delicately branching, feathery antennae *(bottom, near right)*. However, there are exceptions. Skippers' antennae *(top, middle)* are farther apart at the base and end in pointed, curved clubs. Certain moths *(bottom, middle)* have antennae as simple as a butterfly's. Similarly, most butterflies fold their wings at rest *(top, far right)*, while moths spread theirs out *(bottom)*. But there are many exceptions.

Antennae shapes

Perching posture

Butterflies

Swallowtail

Skipper

Hairstreak

Moths

Silkworm moth

Noctuid moth

Adris moth

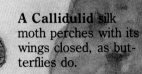

This male hairstreak butterfly of the Lycaenidae family has golden green wings.

A Callidulid silk moth perches with its wings closed, as butterflies do.

The Japanese giant silk moth flies by night, behavior typical of moths.

The Tiger moths of the family Arctiidae are vivid night fliers.

Parnara guttata is a mothlike skipper with a thick abdomen and dun wings.

The Melanidae butterflies are most active around sunset.

At rest the underwing moth conceals its bright orange or yellow hind wings.

Lepidopteran living habits

Moths and butterflies make up the insect order Lepidoptera—whose name means scale-winged. Except for a few moths that have mouths adapted for chewing, adult moths and butterflies live on liquid food—or no food at all. Those that feed take flower nectar up through a tubelike proboscis. Some adults take no food, emerging from their cocoons only to mate and die. Most moths fly by night and can be seen fluttering around street lamps and porch lights. With some exceptions, like the sulphur moth at right, the lepidopterans seen during the day are butterflies.

The sulphur moth is active in daylight.

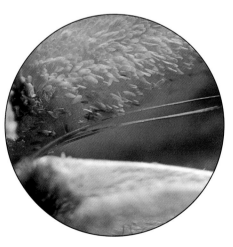

A feature shared by most moths but few butterflies is the frenulum, a thin band of bristles linking the forewing to the hind wing.

33

Can Insects Survive on Ice?

Scientists know of many insects that become dormant at low temperatures, but recently a species of insect was found thriving in the ice and snow of a Himalayan glacier. This insect, the glacier midge, is remarkably resistant to cold and remains active at temperatures below freezing. In fact, it is so well adapted to cold that it cannot survive heat and will die if held in a human hand.

The glacier midge's wings have become too small for flight; it walks over the surface of snow and ice. The developing larvae and pupae live in tunnels where meltwater flows, and they feed on algae and bacteria. Several other species of insect also thrive in cold, snowy environments.

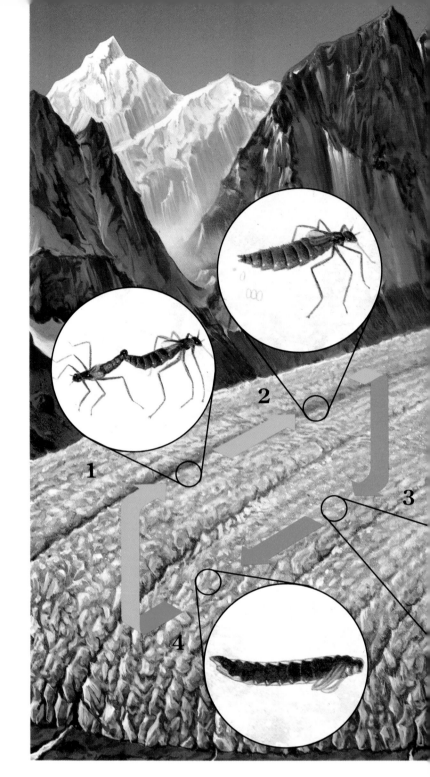

1. Mating. Glacier midges mate in spaces within the ice; the male spends his entire life in the ice.

2. Egg laying. To shield eggs and larvae from strong meltwater flows, the female glacier midge walks upstream to lay eggs.

3. Hatchlings. Glacier-midge larvae venture out of their ice hollows to feed in streams at night.

4. Riding down. As the larvae become pupae *(right)* and adults, the meltwater on the ice carries them downhill.

Cold-weather insects

In addition to the glacier midge, the crane fly and stone fly are active in cold weather and can live in snow. They eat algae and other organic matter in the snow and lay their eggs there.

The stone fly *(far right)* grows to maturity in the cold water beneath the snow. It is active at temperatures as low as 23° F. but cannot survive above 68° F. Such insects can remain active at low temperatures because of the antifreeze-like chemicals in their body fluids.

At home in snow. The crane fly no longer has wings but walks on snow and remains active in temperatures as cold as 14° F.

Ice-age survivor. Immature stages of the stone fly live in mountain streams; then, as adults, they come to the snow's surface to mate and lay eggs.

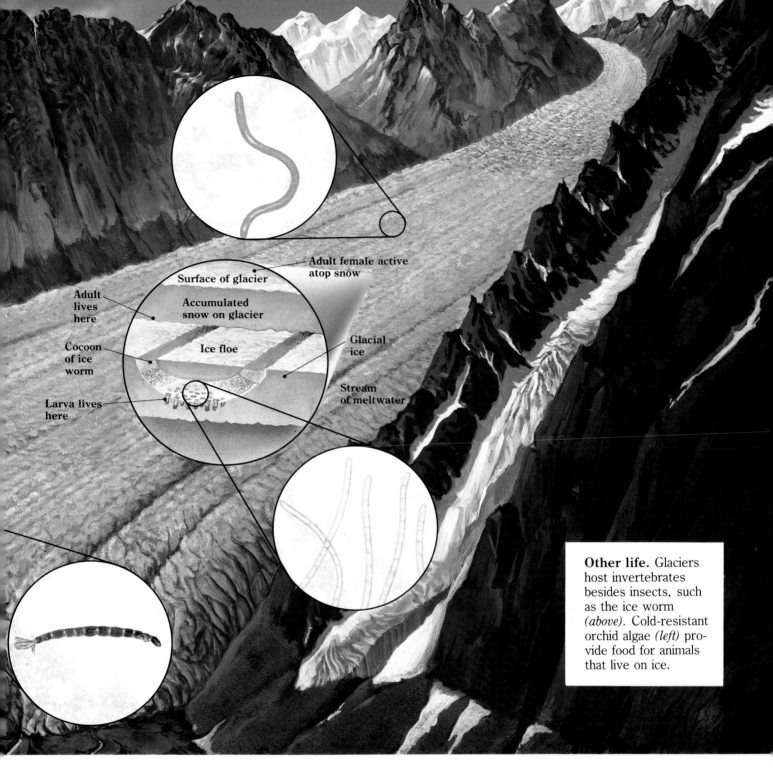

Adult female active
atop snow

Surface of glacier

Accumulated
snow on glacier

Adult
lives
here

Cocoon
of ice
worm

Ice floe

Glacial
ice

Larva lives
here

Stream
of meltwater

Other life. Glaciers
host invertebrates
besides insects, such
as the ice worm
(above). Cold-resistant
orchid algae *(left)* provide food for animals
that live on ice.

Nature's antifreeze

Living cells die when they freeze,
because as water in a cell turns
to ice, it expands, rupturing the
cell membranes *(right, top).* Some
insects survive in freezing weather because they have a natural
antifreeze, called glycerol, in their
body fluids. Their cells do not
freeze until the temperature
drops to −4° F. These protected
cells excrete fluids, so that ice
forms outside the cells *(right,
bottom),* rather than inside. Further protecting the membranes,
the glycerol in these fluids makes
ice crystals form without jagged
edges to damage the cells.

Ordinary cells

Cold-resistant cells

Winterproof pupa. Insects such as the
cabbage butterfly that pass the winter as
pupae *(above)* store glycerol in their body
fluids. Some survive at −22° F.

35

2

Eating Habits

The first insects, developing 350 million years ago, were probably scavengers, nibbling on the remains of dead animals and plants. Their older relatives, the spiders, who go back 400 million years, probably have been predacious from the start. But since then, insects and spiders have diversified enormously. The more than one million insect species and 30,000 spider species have become highly specialized in the foods they eat and the ways in which they get their food.

Spiders entrap their victims. Most insects are plant eaters, but some hunt or stalk prey, and

others lurk in ambush. Even ants may be hunters, sharing their prey with their nest mates through a system of scent communication. Certain mosquito larvae simply turn and gobble up other mosquito larvae.

In many insects, such as the dragonfly larva and praying mantis, body parts have evolved into tools for seizing prey. The larvae of fungus gnats, called glowworms, not only set traps for their prey but lure their victims with a blue light. Some fireflies send false signals to trap other fireflies. And one family of insects, the termites,

uses other organisms to help them digest the wood they eat as they carve out their homes in trees and lumber. This chapter looks at these and other clever methods the insects and spiders have found to feed themselves.

Although they are both arthropods, these animals catch their food in different ways. The spider *(above)* spins a net called an orb web and then waits patiently to capture the insects that stray onto its threads. The dragonfly nymph *(below)* flips out its lower lip with surprising speed to seize its prey.

How Do Spiders Catch Prey?

Some of the world's 30,000 species of spiders catch prey by stalking it or ambushing their victims on the ground. But most spin webs to catch prey in the air. The silk with which they build the webs comes from special organs in their abdomens called spinnerets. Each spider species spins only one kind of web. Some species, like the orb weaver below, coat some of their silk with droplets of sticky liquid. Other species use hundreds of threads of dry silk to build a bewildering maze in which insects lose their way. Different spider tactics are shown at bottom.

Stuck. A butterfly is caught in the sticky web of orb weaver *Argiope bruennichii.* This spider can trap insects as large as grasshoppers.

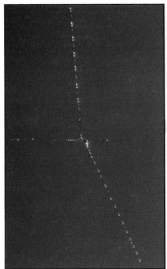

Sticky liquid. Drops of gluey liquid dot the spiral threads but not the spokes of an orb web. Spiders walk on the spokes.

Types of spider webs

Scientists classify spider webs by shapes, some of which are shown at right. Spider webs vary greatly, from a simple line web to the complex, every-which-way jumble of the cobweb. But all are effective for catching prey.

Orb webs. These best-known spider webs are spun by three spider families: the Araneidae, Tetragnathidae, and Uloboridae.

Funnel web. Seen on hedges and trees, this web has a maze to trap insects, which then fall into the flat main web below it.

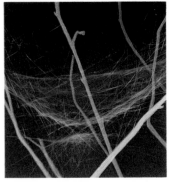

Sheet web. Plate-shaped, flat as a sheet, or domed, these webs are spun among roadside grasses or on the tips of tree branches.

Wrapped up. Feeling its web vibrate, the *Argiope bruennichii* spider rushes to its prey, bites it, and binds it in silk.

Cobweb. The strands of a cobweb may seem haphazard, but the web is actually fairly regular. Some parts are sticky.

Vertical line web. The *Episinus affinis* spider spins two strands and holds them apart, trapping insects on the sticky lower ends.

Line web. This simple web is a line suspended on several threads between tree branches. Some species use sticky thread, others do not.

Spring trap. The triangle spider builds a triangular web, holds the mooring thread, and hauls in the net when prey is caught on it.

39

How Are Mantises Armed for Hunting?

The praying mantis is an insect that ambushes its prey, grabbing it with its special forelegs. The forelegs, seldom used in walking, are not only bowed outward but barbed with spines. Both features help it hold prey securely. The praying mantis is named for the pose it adopts, the tips of its forelegs together, as it waits for small insects to stray within its reach. When a victim gets near enough, the mantis seizes it, pulls it close, and eats it *(far right)*.

The mantis has several other anatomical features that help it in this operation. With its long, narrow thorax, it balances easily among camouflaging stems and branches, holding on with its middle and hind legs. Its compound eyes—so large that they take up most of its head—are aimed left and right, so that by turning its head, the mantis can watch for movement of potential prey over a wide range. The mantis can see only as far as its forelegs can reach. Once it has an appealing insect clearly in view, the mantis suddenly extends its forelegs to make the catch.

How the mantis aims at prey

The praying mantis has a special sensory organ that helps it aim accurately in the direction of its prey. The mantis's head, atop a slender neck, tilts and swivels freely. Along the neck and on the thorax are tiny hair sensilla, which help tell the mantis which direction its head is facing. As the mantis follows its prey with its eyes *(right, middle)*, it turns its head in the direction of the prey *(far right)*. As the head turns, it rubs against the hair sensilla on that side. Sensory cells at the base of these hairs send signals alerting the foreleg on that side to prepare to lash out and capture the prey.

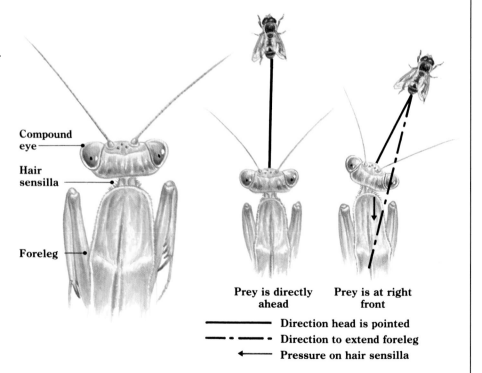

Compound eye

Hair sensilla

Foreleg

Prey is directly ahead

Prey is at right front

—————— Direction head is pointed

— · — · — Direction to extend foreleg

◄—— Pressure on hair sensilla

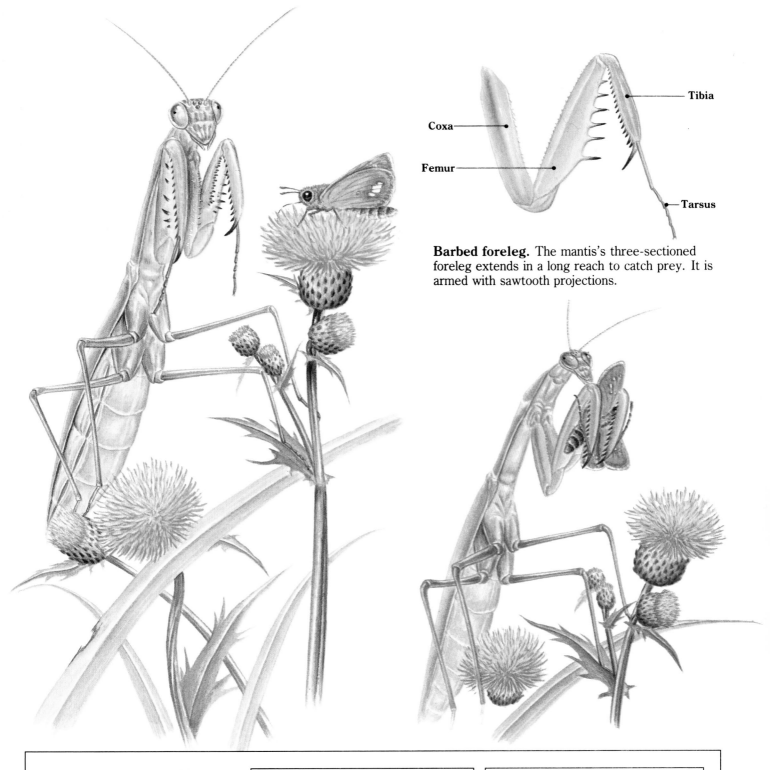

Barbed foreleg. The mantis's three-sectioned foreleg extends in a long reach to catch prey. It is armed with sawtooth projections.

Coxa

Femur

Tibia

Tarsus

Movement when catching prey

When the mantis sees its prey clearly *(1)*, it flips out its foreleg *(2)* and secures the prey by hooking it with the barbs on its tibia and femur *(3 and 4)*. The mantis grabs large prey with both forelegs. While taking aim, the mantis steadies itself on its middle and hind legs, then contracts the muscle that connects the coxa to the thorax. Movement of this muscle makes the foreleg shoot out in a straight line.

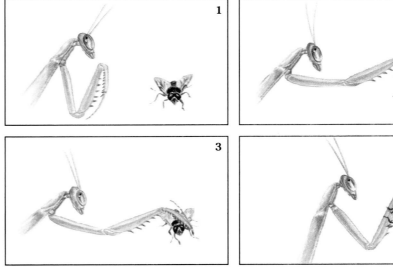

1

2

3

4

How Do Ants Gather Food?

Ants number some 8,800 known species worldwide. They eat a great variety of foods and use different methods to gather them. The black ant, a desert species, for example, is the prudent ant of Aesop's fable: In autumn, it gathers and stores large amounts of grass seed. A different species, the scale ant, uses its mouth as a trap to catch small insects. The ant's long and slender lower jaw, or mandible, swings out sideways and has a long sensory hair projecting from it. The ant waits open-mouthed for prey to come near. When a small insect touches the tip of the sensory hair, the ant's jaw claps shut like a sprung trap, seizing the prey.

Some ants are scavengers, while others are hunters. Certain fire ants hunt small centipedes, and a few gather spider eggs. When fire ants—or other species that live in large colonies—have killed or found fresh food, they signal their nest mates to come and help bring back the food to the nest. To get help, they secrete a trail of scented substance called pheromone. The other ants follow the scent to the food and back again to the nest.

Trailblazing. A fire ant, finding food, lays a pheromone trail to the nest *(below)*. Nest mates follow the scent to the food.

A clear trail of pheromones

Species of fire ants are found throughout tropical and subtropical regions; they are named for the painful, burning stings many species can inflict with their venomous stingers. A fire ant also extends its stinger when it wants to make a trail to lead its nest mates to a fresh food supply. Dragging the barb along the ground as it walks *(opposite, middle),* the worker ant leaves a trail of pheromone, excreted from a gland near the stinger.

A fire ant's pheromone trail can be quickly blown away by breezes across the ground. In one experiment *(right),* a fire ant's 8-inch-long pheromone trail was found to dissipate into the air within 100 seconds—little more than a minute and a half. Because the pheromones dissipate so rapidly, the ants are not confused by old, lingering trails but follow only the freshest trails to the food sources near their nests.

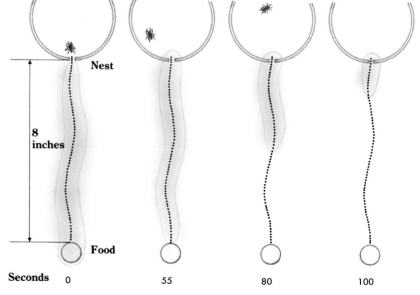

Nest

8 inches

Food

Seconds   0   55   80   100

The exocrine glands of an ant

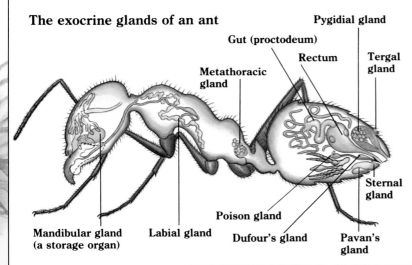

Pygidial gland

Gut (proctodeum)

Rectum

Tergal gland

Metathoracic gland

Sternal gland

Poison gland

Mandibular gland (a storage organ)

Labial gland

Dufour's gland

Pavan's gland

An ant's exocrine system—the glands that send out secretions—includes the glands that produce pheromones for many purposes. Some pheromones trigger mating behavior, while others stimulate ants to defend the nest by fighting invaders. The pheromones most useful in food gathering are the trail pheromones.

These pheromones are secreted by as many as 10 different glands in an ant's body, depending on the species. Fire ants use emissions from the Dufour's gland, near the barb, to lay trails to food. Each worker ant secretes only a tiny amount of pheromone, but a group of ants can lay a lengthy path of odor.

Tandem running to new food

A black carpenter ant that has found food may run to the nest to get help in carrying the food home. Meeting another worker ant, it touches the second ant's head lightly with its antenna and daubs it with a secretion *(right, top)*. The second worker ant, excited by the secretion, quickly falls in line behind the messenger and follows it to its destination. Several kinds of ants use such tandem running, omitting or ignoring pheromone trails. An excited ant will pursue its guide anywhere, even if the "guide" is only a glass rod in the hand of a curious experimenter.

Recruiting a helper

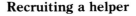

SOS. Returning to the nest, an ant meets a nest mate.

Excitation. The second ant becomes interested.

Marching. The first ant leads the second to its destination.

Odor. The first ant puts a secretion on the other's head.

Following. The ant falls in behind the first ant.

Can Dragonfly Nymphs Catch Fish?

Unlike adult dragonflies, the dragonfly nymph lives underwater and feeds on small aquatic animals, including tadpoles and young fish. It catches prey by suddenly extending its lower lip, which has evolved into a specialized prey-catching device that folds, at rest, underneath its head and thorax. Unfolded, the lip shoots forth in one swift grab, much like the sudden movement of the praying mantis's forelegs *(page 41)*. The nymph tracks its prey not only by looking for it but by sensing vibrations from the movements in the water nearby.

Shooting from the lip

By themselves, the muscles of the nymph's lower lip are not powerful enough to flip out the prey-catching device to its full length. Extra power comes from a local increase of blood, or hemolymph, pressure. When the lip is folded *(near right)*, muscles keep the blood under pressure. When the muscles start extending the lip *(right, center)*, released blood rushes into the articular membranes, adding blood pressure to the lip's movement. The lip cannot "fire" until the blood pressure is high enough.

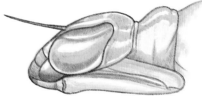

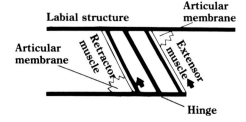

Labial structure

Articular membrane

Articular membrane

Retractor muscle

Extensor muscle

Hinge

At rest. Blood pressure builds at the hinges.

Nice catch. A dragonfly nymph spears a minnow. When the nymph senses prey, it flips out its lower lip in less than ³⁄₁₀₀ of a second.

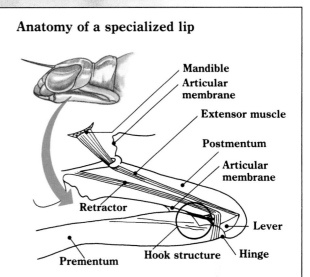

Anatomy of a specialized lip

Mandible
Articular membrane
Extensor muscle
Postmentum
Articular membrane
Retractor
Lever
Hook structure
Hinge
Prementum

The labium, or lip, has two parts, which meet at a hinged joint. Above the joint are two muscles that help extend and flex this lip. Extra power comes from an increase in blood pressure.

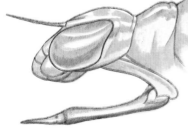

30°

Released. The retractor muscle loosens, and the lip begins to extend.

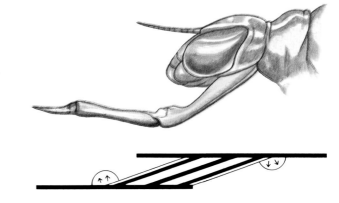

Extended. The articular membranes swell, straightening the lip.

What Are Mosquito Larvae Eating?

Adult female mosquitoes spend much of their time looking for a meal of blood, while the males eat flower nectar. Their young, however, are water dwellers, hatching from eggs laid in ponds and puddles. The larvae hang head downward from the surface of the water, breathing air through tubes near the tip of their abdomens.

A developing mosquito eats nothing during its brief pupal stage *(opposite, bottom),* as it prepares to emerge as an adult. But during its earlier larval stage, it "filter feeds." When the larva draws water into its mouth, constantly moving cilia—brushlike hairs *(below)*—filter out microscopic foodstuff. Mosquito larvae eat algae, molds, bacteria, pollen, small dead water fleas, and plankton. A few species also eat other mosquito larvae.

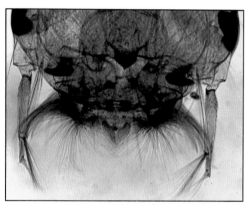

The head. Large antennae and compound eyes nearly fill the mosquito larva's head. With its fuzzy cilia, the larva draws water into its mouth and strains out the edible matter. The cilia flutter between 180 and 240 times per minute, depending on the temperature.

Mosquito life from egg to adult

Eggs of the house mosquito *(right)* are laid on the water's surface in a raft. The eggs hatch the following day, and the larvae begin the first of four larval stages, in which they will molt three times. The larval period lasts about 10 days in water temperatures of 77° F. or warmer. At the end of the fourth larval stage, the shell cracks open and the pupa emerges. The pupa continues to live in water. The female eats nothing while its mouth changes from filter-feeding parts to a bloodsucking siphon. After three or four days, the adult emerges *(far right)* and flies away.

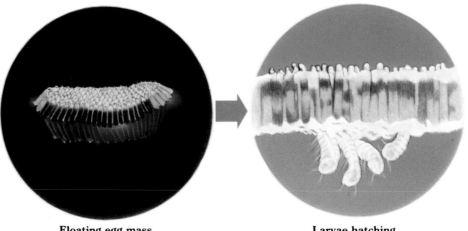

Floating egg mass

Larvae hatching

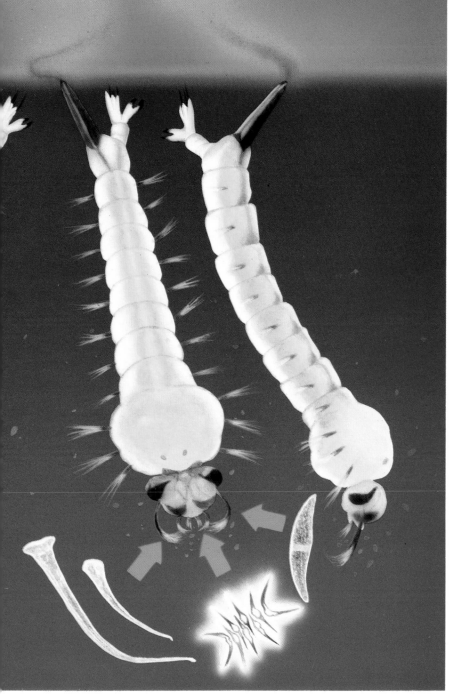

No strain. Hanging head downward in the water, the mosquito larva moves its mouth hairs to draw water into its mouth and eat the organic matter—bacteria, plankton, and the like—that it strains from the water. A larva filters about a quart of water a day.

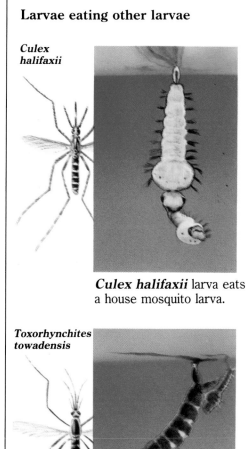

Larvae eating other larvae

Culex halifaxii

Culex halifaxii larva eats a house mosquito larva.

Toxorhynchites towadensis

Toxorhynchites devours an *Aedes* mosquito larva.

In some mosquito species, larvae eat the larvae of other mosquito species and other aquatic insects. But these mosquitoes do not sting; their larvae store enough food energy to lay eggs as adults without ever eating again.

Larvae   Pupa   Emergence as adult

How Do Termites Digest Wood?

Most insects eat the green and living parts of plants—the stems or leaves. But termites eat wood, tunneling through tree trunks and buildings as they construct their homes *(below)*. Wood is mostly dead cells, with little nutritive value, and its components—cellulose, hemicellulose, and lignin—resist digestion. For that reason termites have special ways to digest wood. The higher and lower orders of termites solve the same problem in different ways.

Using fungi as digesters

Many of the higher-order termites raise fungi *(right)* to help them get nutrition from wood. Wood that the termites eat is poorly digested, and much wood is excreted almost intact in their droppings. But these termites use their droppings as food for the fungi that they raise. As the fungi grow, they further break down the wood. Then the termites reconsume their own droppings, together with some of the fungi, and get nourishment from both.

Fungi growing on termites' droppings

Microbes that help digest wood

Lower-order termites rely on microbes called protozoa that live in the termites' intestines *(below, right)* and help them digest wood. The protozoa break down the wood further, turning it into nutrients the termites can absorb. If the microbes in a termite's body die, the termite will die, too.

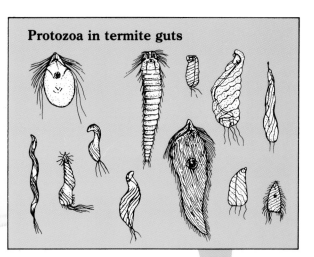

Protozoa in termite guts

Other wood-eating insects

Various insects besides termites eat wood. Some depend, as the lower-order termites do, on microbes in their bodies, but some use other methods. For example, most insect larvae that eat wood also eat the molds or fungi growing on a tree. Scientists believe that the fungi's digestive enzymes assist the insect in digestion.

Some insects do not eat wood directly but raise fungi on the wood as a food source. Such fungi farmers use wood's nutrients indirectly, by eating the fungi.

The long-horned beetle larva eats molds that grow on trees, together with the wood, as it tunnels its way through a tree trunk.

Bark beetles lay eggs under a tree's bark, dropping fungus spores from a special fold as they burrow. When the larvae hatch, they live on the fungi.

49

Why Do Glowworms Glow?

Glowworms of Australia and New Zealand are not worms at all. They are the larvae of fungus gnats. In their larval stage—which lasts 10 months—the insects look like inch-long worms and live in tubular sheaths that they build and attach to cave roofs, riverbanks, and fallen logs.

The glowworm is named for the pale blue light it emits from the tip of its abdomen. Its light organs are at the end of the Malpighian tubules, specialized parts of the alimentary canal, through which body waste passes. The light, shining continuously in the gloom of caves, attracts small insects.

To trap the midges and flies it lures, each glowworm spins 20 to 30 silk threads, adds a sticky substance from its mouth, and hangs the threads from its sheath. An insect flying toward the glowworm's light is likely to bump into a dangling thread and stick to it. Once an insect is caught, the glowworm reels in the thread and eats its prey.

Sheath building and line hanging

Each larva has a mucus gland, which secretes a clear mucus, and a silk gland, which spins thread. The larva starts its sheath with a layer of mucus, securing it to the cave roof with silk threads. Using additional mucus, the larva enlarges its sheath to perhaps five times its body length. The larva hangs its "fishing lines"—the dangling threads with their beads of mucus (*right*)—from the threads that fasten the sheath to the roof. The larva always lies on its back in its sheath.

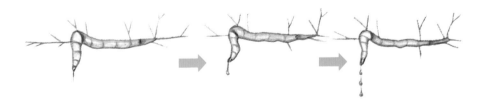

Leaning out of the sheath, the glowworm drops thread and mucus together.

Next the larva emits only thread, lowering the droplet on the thread.

The larva secretes mucus again to add another sticky bead to the thread.

The adult fungus gnat

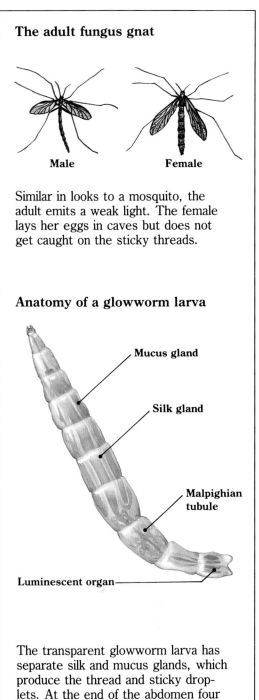

Male   **Female**

Similar in looks to a mosquito, the adult emits a weak light. The female lays her eggs in caves but does not get caught on the sticky threads.

Anatomy of a glowworm larva

Mucus gland

Silk gland

Malpighian tubule

Luminescent organ

The transparent glowworm larva has separate silk and mucus glands, which produce the thread and sticky droplets. At the end of the abdomen four Malpighian tubules form a thick light-producing structure.

Snagged prey is reeled in

By sensing vibration in one of its dangling lines, the larva knows when prey is caught and where. The larva then stretches out head-first to follow the vibrating thread down. When half of its body leans from the sheath *(right),* the glow-worm starts reeling in the thread, holding the rolled-up line under its body while stretching out for a fresh grip. When it has hoisted the prey up to its mouth, the glow-worm bites the insect and pulls it into the sheath.

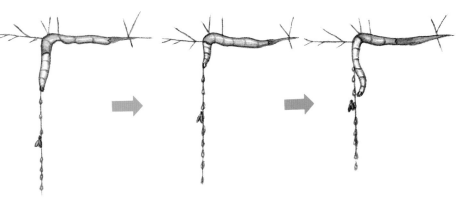

Taking the line in its mouth, the larva begins to reel it in.

Contracting the front half of its body, it pulls up the thread.

Pulling further, the glowworm closes in on its prey.

Are Some Fireflies Prey for Others?

Signaling. Two male *Photinus* fireflies send light flashes in a special pattern. Each seeks a female with whom to mate.

Courting. The *Photinus* female glows on the ground, signaling in response to the flashes of males of her species.

Mating. Attracted by the light of the responding *Photinus* female, the *Photinus* male nears. Once the pair confirm that both belong to the same species, they mate.

Fireflies twinkle in the twilight in many parts of the world. Both male and female fireflies emit their light as a mating signal, but females generally wait on the ground, while males fly about looking for them. Each species has a distinctive signal pattern, enabling fireflies to find mates of the same species and avoid interbreeding, which would yield sterile offspring.

But some fireflies mimic the light signals of other fireflies, catching and eating members of other species that are tricked by this mimicry. One of these is North America's *Photuris*. Once the female *Photuris* has mated with a male of her species, she sends light flashes that attract males of other species. When an interested male arrives, she catches and devours him *(below)*.

He is deceived. One *Photinus* male sees a firefly's light flashing in the pattern used by receptive *Photinus* females. But the signal comes from the *Photuris* female.

He is devoured. When he alights, the hopeful *Photinus* male finds only the *Photuris* female, an insect much larger than himself. She catches him and eats him.

Can a Small Wasp Defeat a Big Spider?

Although the spider wasp lives on flower nectar, the female provides large spiders for her larvae to eat. She manages this feat by paralyzing a spider much larger than she is with a sting from her poisonous barb *(right)*. She then digs a tunnel, places the paralyzed spider at the bottom, and lays an egg on top of it *(opposite, bottom)*. The spider will still be alive, harmless and edible, a few days later when the young wasp hatches and needs food.

The spider wasp is one of several species of hunting wasps who use spiders, crickets, and other insects this way. One wasp, the *Pepsis* of the southwestern United States, takes on 5-inch-wide tarantulas—and wins.

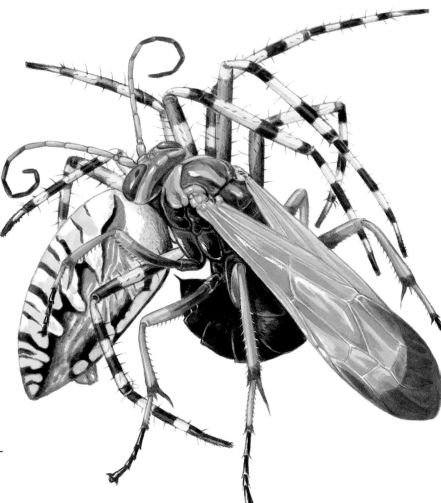

The sting. Knocked to the ground, the spider is at a disadvantage and struggles to escape. The wasp pins the spider on its back. Standing on her hind legs and curling her own abdomen forward, the wasp delivers a paralyzing sting to the spider's abdomen.

New food supply. A spider wasp stings a *Dolomedes sulfureus*. She will bury the spider alive and lay an egg on it.

On the shelf. Collecting a paralyzed spider from a leaf, the spider wasp prepares to store it in her burrow.

The attack. The spider tries to defend itself against the attacking wasp but cannot scare the wasp away. At last the wasp knocks the spider out of the web.

Invading the web. The spider wasp challenges an *Argiope amoena* spider, provoking it by standing in the center of the spider's web. The wasp advances and backs off repeatedly.

The nest. The wasp drags or flies the spider, which can be twice her own weight, to her nesting site. She drops the paralyzed, live spider nearby and begins to dig, occasionally checking the spider to make sure ants do not steal it.

The birth chamber. When the burrow is dug, the wasp pushes the spider to the bottom of it. She then lays her egg on the spider's abdomen, fills in the burrow, and hides the entrance with sand or wood chips. When the egg hatches, the larva will feed on the tissues of the spider.

3

Life Cycles of Insects

Insect life begins in the egg. Laid singly or in clusters of up to several thousand, the eggs are usually fertilized by a male, but sometimes the eggs develop without the benefit of sperm. Insect eggs incubate in various places: in the ground or within protective capsules, atop bodies of water or attached to leaves or twigs. Eggs of parasitic insects may have been deposited on or within the body of another insect or an animal host. Development from the egg proceeds in two main stages. In complete metamorphosis, larvae, which may bear no resemblance to the adult

insect, emerge from the eggs. The wormlike larvae gradually develop rudimentary wings and eyes, and after the last larval molt, enter the pupal stage, which they usually spend in a sacklike cocoon. Immobilized for a time, the pupa eventually splits open its tiny prison to emerge as an adult. In incomplete metamorphosis, the larvae may appear as miniature versions of the adult, called nymphs. As larvae grow, they must shed their hard outer shell, or exoskeleton. These moltings happen once or dozens of times before adulthood. The adult insect might live only for a few days or weeks. Some insects, like aphids, produce several generations each year, while others, notably the periodical cicada, take years to complete their life cycles.

During its metamorphosis a swallowtail butterfly *(above)* transforms into a number of different shapes. Although the grasshopper *(below)* also goes through metamorphosis, it changes less profoundly during its development from nymph to adult.

How Do Cabbage Whites Select Mates?

In a zigzagging flight *(green line)*, a male cabbage white butterfly searches for a female with which to mate. Undeterred by another male nearby, he descends to approach a likely candidate.

Unmated females hold their wings upright, displaying the pale coloring of their undersides.

Separating sexes by color

In natural light, male *(left)* and female *(right)* cabbage whites appear similar from top and bottom.

An ultraviolet filter reveals that cabbage whites see males as dusky *(left)*, females as pale on top *(right)*.

The wing color of male and female cabbage whites differs because of special pigments called pteridines, which vary in intensity between the sexes. The females' wings are rich in pteridines. Seen by butterfly eyes, which pick up ultraviolet wavelengths that are shorter than visible light wavelengths, the pteridines have a pale cast.

A male cabbage white butterfly *(Pieris rapae crucivora)* begins the search for a mate almost immediately after emerging from his cocoon. Attracted to plants in the cabbage family, he flutters among the leaves looking for females. To his eyes, which see not only visible but also ultraviolet light, the wings of females appear white, whereas those of males look much darker. Spotting a potential partner, a male drops down and attempts to mate.

Among other butterfly species, males may also be guided to mates by the scent of pheromones, which are released into the air. Moths, which cannot see well, rely on such clues.

The male cabbage white *(magnified, above)* is able to find females even if his antennae are damaged or missing. The butterfly relies only little on touch or smell to locate his mates but depends largely on sight.

Cabbage whites mate back to back. The female lays her eggs on cabbage leaves.

In the experiment above, a piece of paper brushed with ultraviolet paint is as alluring to a male cabbage white as a female would be, confirming that males respond to certain visual clues to find mates.

Saying no, butterfly style

Wings lowered and abdomen curled, an already-mated female rejects advances from a male.

Clear lens over eye

Blackened lens over eye

Lens removed

Rejection posture

Receptive posture

Rejection posture

An experiment confirms that females, too, respond to visual stimuli. When an already-mated female *(far left)* has her eyes covered by a clear lens, she maintains a rejecting posture. With a blackened lens *(middle)*, her posture becomes receptive. The lens removed *(near left)*, she again strikes a discouraging pose, wings dropped and abdomen raised.

59

Why Do Some Beetles Have Horns?

A Hercules beetle, at nearly 7 inches long the world's largest beetle *(below, right),* locks spiny horns around a rival, attempting to overturn it.

Battling male rhinoceros beetles butt horns. Each attempts to slip a prong beneath the thorax of the other. The victor uses its horn to flip the loser. Once a beetle is on its back, it is defenseless.

● **The mating game**

Among most beetle species, females congregate where food, such as tree sap, is plentiful. At the food site, they attract males by releasing a chemical known as a mating pheromone. Males fresh from victory in battle arrive to court and mate with females. Some males hold females down with their horn while mating, as the rhinoceros beetle shown at right is doing. Mating goes on from late summer into fall. Females then lay eggs in rotting logs, piles of dung, or burrows. The eggs hatch into larvae for the winter, then metamorphose into pupae and grow to adulthood by summer.

Beetles, the most numerous order of insects, come in a wide array of sizes, shapes, and colors. Among their most impressive attributes are the prominent horns that are sported by some male beetles. Charles Darwin, the principal author of the theory of evolution, was one of the first naturalists to comment on the horns, which are more than mere decoration. Beetles wield their horns as fearsome and effective weapons in battles over food, territory, or females . The horns vary in length and shape among species of beetles. Some species use their horns like pincers, others like levers, and still others like lances. Combat with horns can be violent and even fatal, so smaller males, though armed, often avoid conflict when possible.

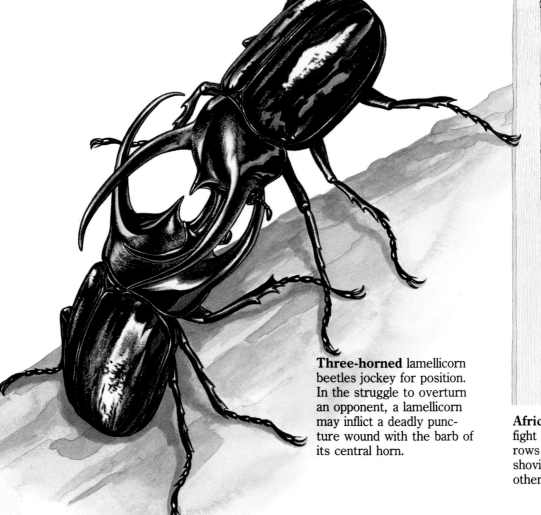

Three-horned lamellicorn beetles jockey for position. In the struggle to overturn an opponent, a lamellicorn may inflict a deadly puncture wound with the barb of its central horn.

African Hercules beetles fight over possession of burrows in sugarcane stalks, shoving and gripping each other with viselike horns.

The strategy of the small male

Unable to hold their own in battle, smaller males of many beetle species have found a good method for acquiring both food and mates. They skirt the combat zone by flying to feeding stations early in the evening. There they are able to mate hurriedly with females before larger males descend. Near right, a small-horned male wings toward a sap-laden tree. Next, a female prepares to land, and the small-horned male succeeds in mating with her. A large-horned male approaches and settling on the tree, chases off the smaller male. At far right, larger males dominate.

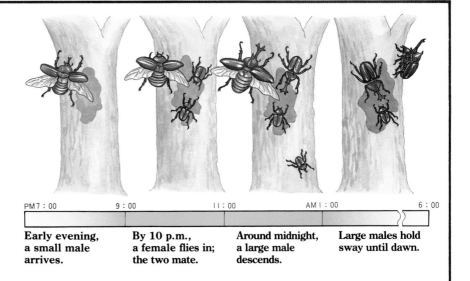

PM 7 : 00   9 : 00   11 : 00   AM 1 : 00   6 : 00

Early evening, a small male arrives.

By 10 p.m., a female flies in; the two mate.

Around midnight, a large male descends.

Large males hold sway until dawn.

How Do Dragonflies Mate?

Ancient in evolutionary terms, dragonflies, in the order of Odonata, were among the first insects to fly. Fitted with two sets of lacy wings and brilliantly colored bodies, they flit and hover over ponds and streams. At mating time, they couple while either airborne or perched on a plant stem. Some spend a few seconds, others several hours, in the air mating in a "wheel position," with the female hanging upside down from the male's abdomen. Often, after a female's eggs have been fertilized, the male continues to fly with her until the eggs are deposited, which guards against mating attempts by other males. Eggs hatch into aquatic larvae, which may take as long as five years to mature.

Dance of the dragonfly

Mating of dragonflies begins when a male flies over an airborne female and grasps her with his legs.

Having obtained from the male's pouch a store of sperm, which fertilizes the eggs she holds in an egg sac, the female disengages to lay her eggs under the pond's surface. Meanwhile, the hovering male may mate with other females nearby.

While the male holds on to a blade of grass, the female wraps her legs around him and bends her abdomen to touch his sperm-filled pouch.

A male's claspers operate like pliers. In some species, females have indentations behind the head that help hold claspers in place.

In a skilled aerial maneuver, the male takes the female by the neck with his tail claspers and unloosens his legs. The pair move along together.

Having previously filled a genital pouch at the front of his abdomen with sperm from reproductive organs at the tip of his tail, the male steers the female to a suitable spot for mating at the pond's edge.

Three ways to lay eggs

The male may remain attached to the mated female while she releases her eggs into the water.

A female goes on alone after mating, poking her tail into mud or water to deposit the eggs.

Diving underwater, the pair cling to a plant where the female affixes her eggs.

In the wheel position

Damselflies have mating rituals similar to those of dragonflies, with the male clasping the female behind the neck, while she curls her abdomen toward him *(right)*. Smaller than dragonflies, damselflies have a thin body and can close their wings at rest, whereas dragonflies hold their wings open. Both dragonflies and damselflies lay their eggs in water, where the young develop into nymphs.

Do Praying Mantises Eat Their Mates?

Praying mantises are known for a strange mating ritual. The females are said to behead and devour their partners before, during, or after mating. In fact, more often than not, males avoid being eaten through a combination of caution and speed. Creeping up on the larger female from behind, a male clasps the female's thorax, then mates. When he is finished, he scurries off, avoiding the female's powerful forelegs. Only if the male errs in his approach or lingers after mating does the female attempt to grab him with her pincers and eat him. Scientists speculate that this behavior ensures that only the fleetest and stealthiest male mantises reproduce and pass on desirable traits to offspring. However, even when males have lost their heads during mating, their reflexes continue and they complete the act, which has led some scientists to suggest that the prime reason for this cannibalism is the females' need for extra nourishment for the eggs.

4 Having delivered his sperm, the male hurries out of range of the female's deadly grasp. In general, mantises are solitary insects, and the female lays her eggs alone, dropping 10 to 400 of them in a spongy substance that hardens when exposed to air.

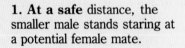

● Caution is key

Since females may mistake a potential mate for dinner, males engage in a careful courtship routine. Normally, praying mantises take on their characteristic pose, with forelegs folded against the long upper section of the thorax and body gently swaying, when encountering prey. Here, the stance is both watchful and defensive. Males proceed from this stage gradually to the point of mating.

1. At a safe distance, the smaller male stands staring at a potential female mate.

2. Making sure he has encountered the proper female, the male leaps and displays his wings to signal his intentions.

4. The female charges yet lifts her tail receptively.

5. The male circles behind, angling to take her unawares.

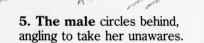

Mantis reproduction rites

1 Stealth is vital if the male is to survive his quest to mate with the violent female.

2 Pouncing, the male reaches for the lower part of the female's thorax.

3 Having eluded the female's grasp, the male lowers his abdomen and mates with her.

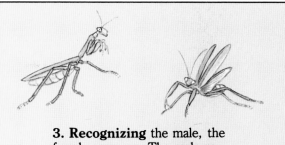

3. Recognizing the male, the female rears up. The male remains safely out of reach.

6. To mate successfully, the male must face forward.

An unlucky suitor

A female praying mantis munches on her hapless mate in the photograph at right. This male failed to survive the courtship. Although carnivorous females may consume mates, cannibalism is more the exception than the rule. The female will probably bear offspring sired by this male, because he continued to mate even after losing his head. Larval mantises resemble their parents, although with only rudimentary wings. They feed on other insects and spiders.

What Is Gift Giving among Insects?

To win acceptance, some male insects present potential mates with nuptial gifts during courtship. Generally, the gifts take the form of food but may also merely be empty packages designed to stimulate the female's interest or divert her attention during mating. Before searching for a mate, many male flies kill prey, then enclose the remains in cases made from silk or a frothy secretion. Carrying the lightweight cases to a mating site, the males pass them to females, which clasp the gifts to their abdomens. While she is occupied, the female all but ignores the male as he proceeds to couple with her. Among more advanced species, males present only empty cases or bits of petals or leaves, which serve the same purpose.

A male scorpionfly inserts his needlelike proboscis into a raspberry to suck its juice. Berry juice is the female's preferred food.

Defensive presents

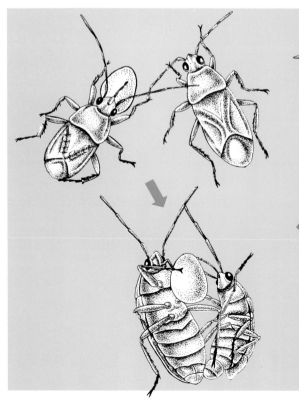

A male stink bug steadies a seed by threading his proboscis into it *(far left)*. A female stink bug arrives and mimics him *(far left, bottom)*. The male gives her the seed and fertilizes her eggs while she is preoccupied with the seed *(below)*.

Attracted by the smell of the berry, a female lands on a stem nearby, signaling her interest in the food.

The willing male cedes his place to the female. While she feeds, he positions himself in such a way that he can grasp her abdomen with his tail pincers and mate with her until she stops eating.

The carnivorous female dance fly of the family Empididae may attack her suitors. To divert her, the male brings gifts of food.

A male hanging scorpionfly clings to a twig while mating with a female who is feeding on his offering of a fly. Only if the male's gift is large enough will the female mate with him.

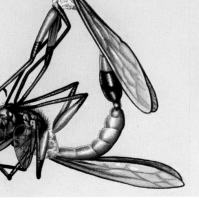

Why Do Mosquitoes Suck Blood?

Some adult female mosquitoes, members of the Culicidae family of insects, require a diet of mammalian blood to nourish their fertilized eggs. For this reason, they have evolved specialized physical machinery. Alighting on a likely victim—here a human being—the mosquito deploys her proboscis, steadied by the labium, hunting for a good place to sting. Within the sheath of the proboscis are six sharp probes, called stylets, that pierce the skin. Once a capillary has been struck, a hollow probe called the labrum functions like a pipe. Another probe, the hypopharynx, sluices saliva into the hole, thinning the blood and preventing it from coagulating (this saliva is what causes the itchiness of mosquito bites). Creating suction with two powerful mouth pumps, the mosquito pulls blood up through the labrum *(red)* into her mouth and onward directly into the midgut. Within two or three minutes, the insect fills her "tank." Fully loaded, engorged to more than twice her normal weight, she lumbers slowly into the air. The mosquito remains sluggish for some time while the blood is digested. One meal is enough to nourish 300 eggs.

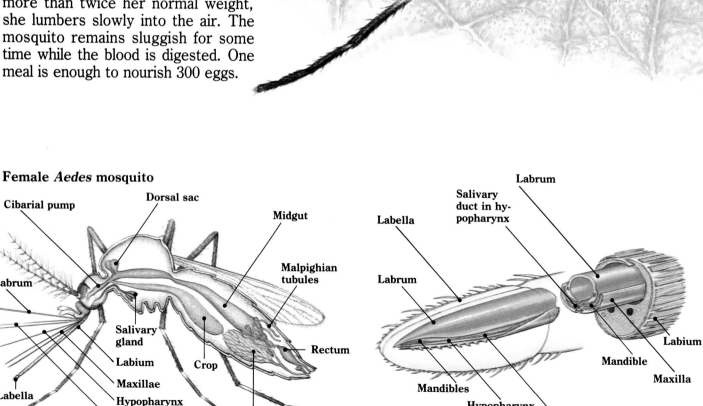

Female *Aedes* mosquito

Cibarial pump · Dorsal sac · Midgut · Malpighian tubules · Labrum · Salivary gland · Labium · Maxillae · Hypopharynx · Mandibles · Labella · Crop · Ovary · Rectum

Labrum · Salivary duct in hypopharynx · Labella · Labrum · Labium · Mandible · Maxilla · Mandibles · Hypopharynx · Maxilla

A mosquito's complex digestive tract includes the salivary gland, dorsal sac, crop and midgut, Malpighian tubules, and rectum.

The labium, or lower lip, and the six stylets—the two mandibles, two maxillae, hypopharynx with salivary duct, and the labrum—form the proboscis.

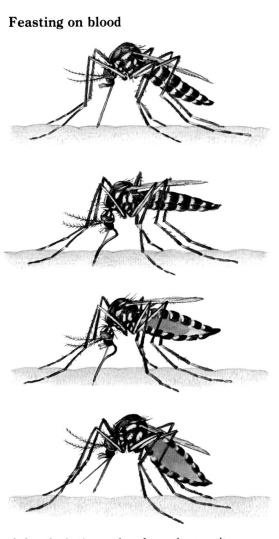

A female *(top)* searches for a site to sting, then pierces the skin with a pair of maxillae. Blood flows up through the labrum *(middle pictures)* and is sucked into the midgut by pumps. Once full, the mosquito withdraws her proboscis and prepares to fly away *(bottom)*.

Eggs that thrive on blood

Before sucking blood

After sucking blood

Maturing eggs

Maturing eggs

Matured eggs

Sugary liquids like nectar, upon which mosquitoes feed as well, flow into the crop *(orange)*. But blood is sent to the midgut *(green)*, where it is digested and absorbed and will ultimately provide nutrients for the eggs.

Raftlike eggs of *Culex* mosquitoes, magnified in this photo, are laid on the surface of bodies of water.

How Do Honeybees Reproduce?

Within colonies of honeybees *(Apis mellifera)*, much activity centers on the laying, tending, and hatching of eggs. In the hive, a single queen with an oversize abdomen spends her life depositing eggs—both unfertilized and fertilized—in special cells of the honeycomb. Unfertilized eggs develop into males, called drones, which will mate with a future queen. Depending on their treatment, larvae hatched from fertilized eggs develop into either queens or female workers. The workers build honeycombs, forage for pollen and nectar, and tend larvae. In mating with numerous drones, a young queen receives a life's supply of sperm, which is stored in a sac called a spermatheca. Once her supply is used up, the colony kills the old queen and nurtures a new one.

Sizing up a nursery's cells

A queen bee measures a cell with her forelegs before releasing an egg, which travels from the ovary down the tubelike oviduct. Sperm from the spermatheca flows down another duct. Her eggs issue from a valve near the stinger.

Worker-bee nursery

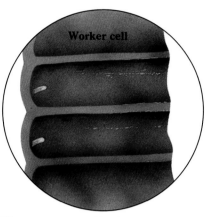

The narrow cells, in cross section above, hold eggs that will develop into worker-bee larvae.

Drone nursery

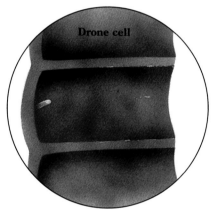

Unfertilized eggs go into the large cells of the drone nursery.

Royal nursery

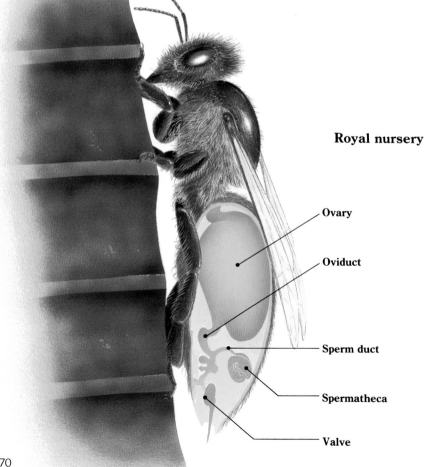

Ovary

Oviduct

Sperm duct

Spermatheca

Valve

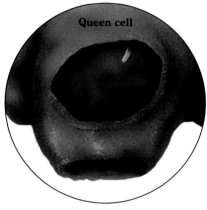

Occupying the largest cell, this egg will mature into a queen.

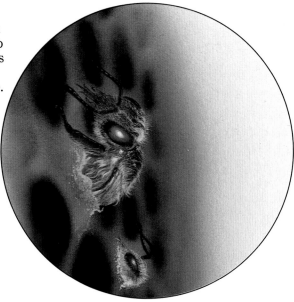

Newly molted worker bees break through the protective wax cap of their cells. The cells are capped when larvae mature into pupae. From egg to adult, worker bees develop in about 21 days.

When the larva hatches, worker nurse bees feed it with pollen and a mixture of fluids produced in the workers' glands.

A drone needs more time to develop than either queen or worker, remaining a day or two longer in the larval and pupal stages.

An adult drone, outweighing queens and worker bees, emerges after about 23 days. The male reproductive organs of a drone produce sperm to fertilize the queen's eggs, fulfilling the major function of drones.

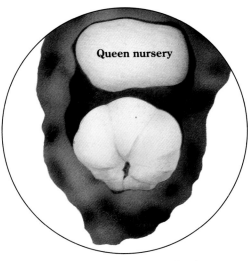

A queen bee larva first feeds on royal jelly, a protein-rich food secreted by workers' glands that is later supplemented with honey.

A queen emerges from her spacious chamber. For the first three days, worker and queen larvae are interchangeable, but after that a plentiful diet boosted by special hormones produces the characteristics of a queen.

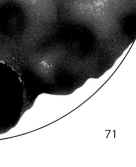

How Are Aphids Born?

Aphids, also known as plant lice, are soft-bodied insects that belong to the Aphididae family. Most species of aphids begin their life cycles in early spring, when eggs hatch into wingless females. These females feed on plant sap and, without mating with males, soon produce one or two broods of live-born young. The second and third generations may be wingless females who eventually give birth to winged females. In many species, these winged females will migrate from their host plant to an alternate plant and give birth to winged females. By fall, the winged females return to the host plant and give birth to wingless females who in turn will mate with winged males that were produced by the females on the second host plant. They deposit eggs on plant twigs or leaves, where the eggs will spend the winter. In the course of feeding, aphids devastate their host plants, often entire fields.

The aphid's annual round

3 Winged females fly away to feed on an alternate host plant. The aphids pictured here prefer plants in the cabbage family.

2 Still on the peach tree, a second generation of wingless females gives birth to live females with wings *(left)*.

Move from peach tree to eggplant

Summer

4 While feeding on the second host plant, winged females produce wingless females and males *(below)*. Badly infested plants wither or die.

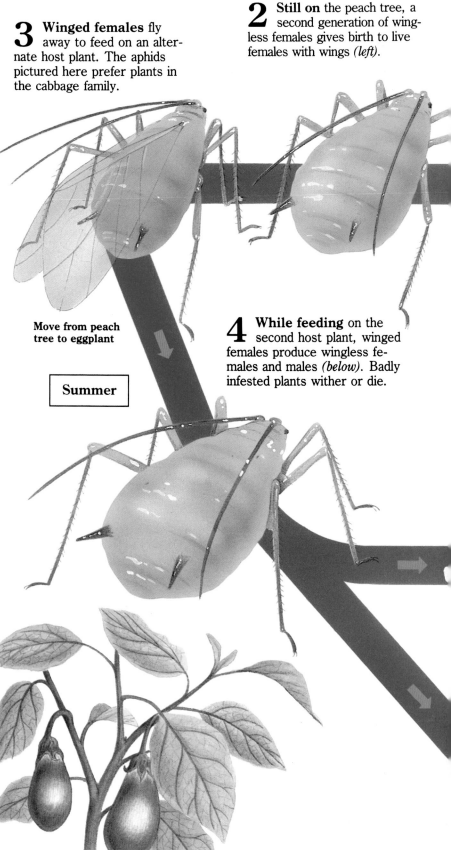

A female aphid gives birth *(above)*. In spring and summer, aphids bear live young. These garden pests multiply rapidly, feeding on many valuable crops. Each species tends to prefer a different type of plant. Their sticky excretion, called honeydew, damages plants by encouraging the growth of molds.

1 **In spring,** a wingless female hatches from an egg laid on a peach tree and begins giving birth to wingless females without mating first.

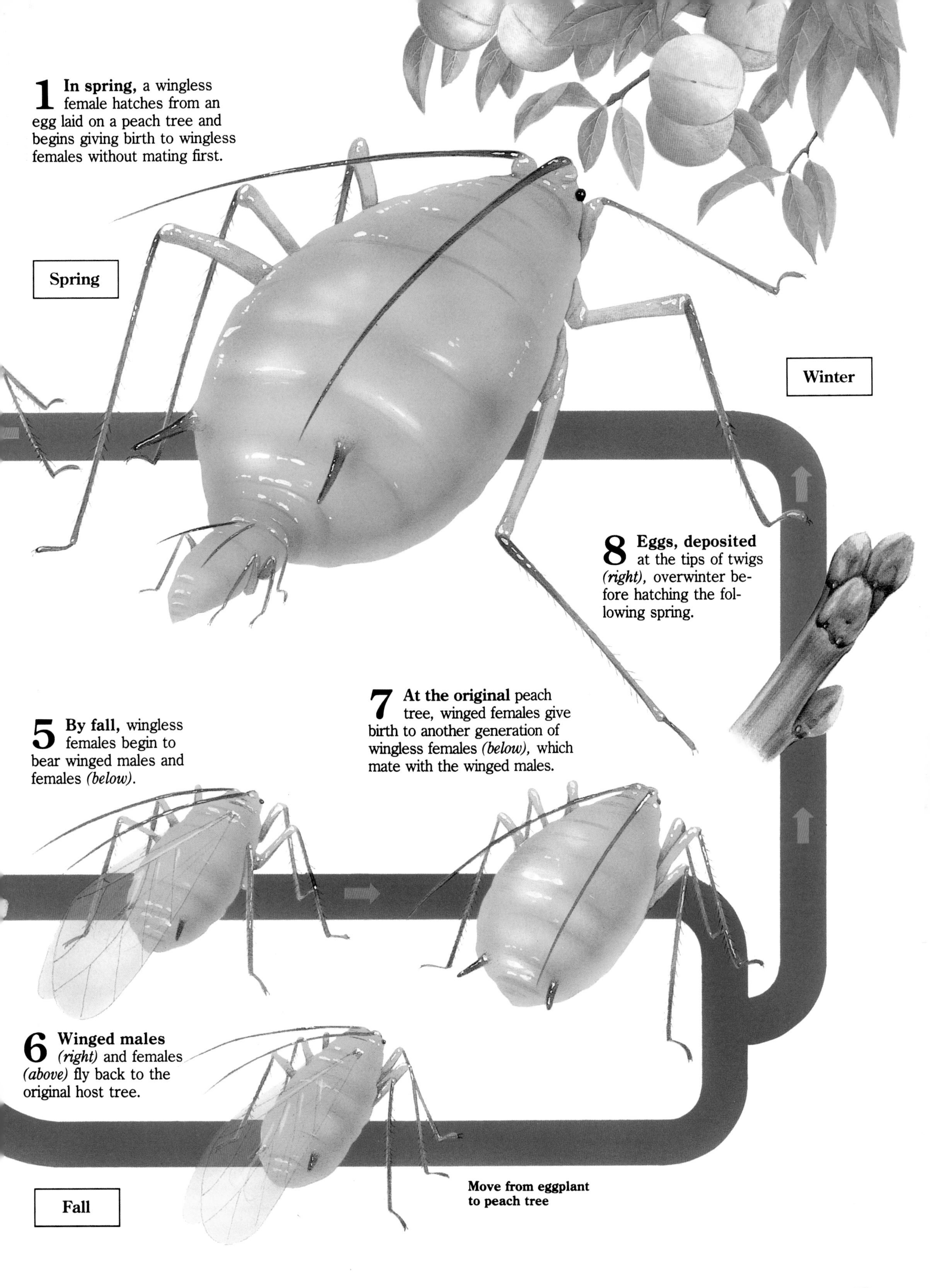

Spring

Winter

8 **Eggs, deposited** at the tips of twigs *(right)*, overwinter before hatching the following spring.

7 **At the original** peach tree, winged females give birth to another generation of wingless females *(below)*, which mate with the winged males.

5 **By fall,** wingless females begin to bear winged males and females *(below)*.

6 **Winged males** *(right)* and females *(above)* fly back to the original host tree.

Move from eggplant to peach tree

Fall

Do Bugs Care for Their Young?

Insects, spiders, and their relatives can be attentive parents. Some species guard their eggs from predators, provide nourishment to larvae, or herd newly hatched offspring. Females generally carry out these tasks, although males share the responsibilities on occasion. Once eggs are laid, they may be endangered by other creatures seeking food, by the growth of molds and fungi, or by harsh weather conditions. To protect them, parents shield the eggs with their bodies, remove mold spores from them, or provide a steady supply of moisture by dipping eggs into a pond. Once eggs are hatched, parents attack or divert predators, signal alarms, or carry nymphs out of harm's way.

1. The purple hairstreak, one of the few butterflies to guard their eggs, rests beside several hundred eggs deposited under a leaf.

2. A wolf spider carries a mass of young on its back as it goes about its day in search of food.

3. A female earwig, of the order Dermaptera—once wrongly thought to crawl in people's ears—keeps mold and fungus from growing on her eggs.

4. A female burrowing cricket (*Anurogryllus muticus*) guards two nymphs hatched inside a sealed, grass-floored brood chamber.

5. A common sawfly, of the Tenthredinidae family, oversees its eggs. Once hatched, the larvae eat the leaves of trees and shrubs while a parent hovers nearby.

6. Spinning silk strands, the poisonous *Cheiracanthium japonicum* spider sews a grass blade into a nest for eggs. Upon hatching, the young devour their mother.

7. A mother scorpion carries her young, born live, on her back. Eventually, the young leave at night to hunt insects and spiders.

8. In some species of giant water bug of the Belostomatidae family, a male ferries eggs around on his back until they hatch. The females compete for males on which to lay eggs.

9. The giant water bug *(Lethocerus americanus)* wets a mass of eggs with pondwater. If allowed to dry out by inattentive parents, eggs will not hatch.

How Do Pill Bugs Tend Their Young?

Pill bugs, or sow bugs, are not insects; while part of the great phylum of arthropods, which includes insects, they belong to a group of creatures, such as lobsters and crabs, called crustaceans. They can be found worldwide from steamy jungles to arid deserts, in mountains as well as low-lying coastal areas. Although highly adaptable, pill bugs retain remnants of their oceanic origins, requiring water to live. Many species gravitate to damp forest floors or rocky shorelines. Some even breathe through gills. The essential chore of pill bug parents is to provide helpless offspring with moisture. Females carry eggs on the underside of their abdomens in a fluid-filled sac until hatching. The young, closely resembling adults, break free and almost immediately begin scavenging for food.

The tender white bodies of newly hatched pill bugs *(inset, right)* are highly vulnerable. To keep them from harm, the mother pill bug watches over her young for a short time after they hatch. If threatened, pill bugs roll into a ball. This defensive posture has the added benefit of conserving moisture.

Maternal care in pill bug kin

The female centipede *(near right)* and scorpion *(far right)*, both related to pill bugs, also show maternal tendencies. Centipedes lay clusters of eggs and carry them until they mature, licking them frequently to remove mold. Nocturnal scorpions bear live young, which ride piggyback for a time. There the young are protected from predators by the fearsome tail stinger of the mother, which contains a poison deadly to insects and small animals.

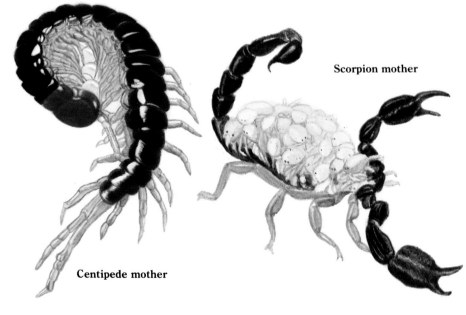

Scorpion mother

Centipede mother

Egg mass

Ecology in a petri dish

Pill bugs are efficient scavengers, as shown in the experiment below. At left, pill bugs begin feeding on a dead leaf. As they decimate the leaf and digest the material, their droppings *(center and right)* are the first step in recycling matter. In nature, these droppings would be further broken down by microbes until they resembled soil. Through these digestive processes, pill bugs play a vital role in soil formation.

Day one　　　　　　　**Day two**　　　　　　　**Day five**

What Is Coevolution between Insects?

Scientists use the term *coevolution* to refer to relationships that have developed over time—perhaps millions of years—between two species of insects, or insects and plants, or between predators and their prey. Coevolved insects behave in ways that complement each other, as in the examples of symbiosis shown below and at right among ants and butterflies. Colonies of certain species of ant herd, transport, and defend some species of butterfly. In return, ants may eat a sweet liquid produced by the butterflies, although in some cases, butterfly larvae turn against them and feed on ant larvae.

Butterflies raised by ants

Large blue butterfly

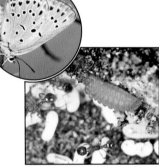

Sievers blue

Japanese copper

Hairstreak

Dozens of Lycaenid butterfly species have evolved relationships with ants. Four such species are depicted above, shown during caterpillar and adult stages *(circular insets)*. Large blues and coppers are raised by ants of the Myrmica genus, which carry caterpillars to the nest and are later consumed by them. Hairstreaks migrate to nests of ants of the *Cremato-gaster* genus, where they are nourished as they grow but are also sometimes eaten by the ants. *Niphanda fusca* butterflies and black ants have a type of symbiotic relationship called mutualism *(right)*, in which both species benefit.

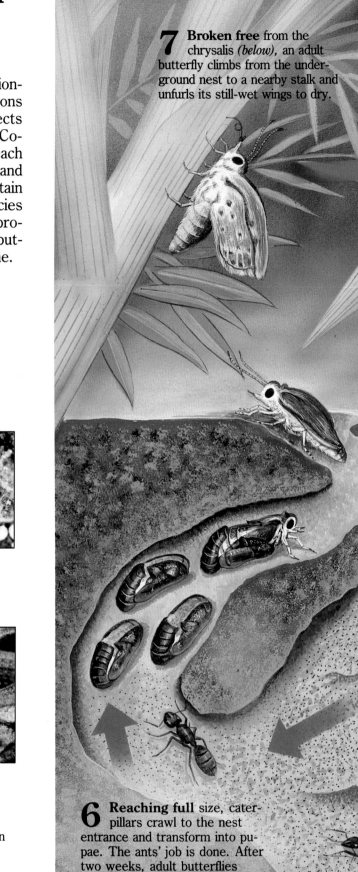

7 **Broken free** from the chrysalis *(below)*, an adult butterfly climbs from the underground nest to a nearby stalk and unfurls its still-wet wings to dry.

6 **Reaching full** size, caterpillars crawl to the nest entrance and transform into pupae. The ants' job is done. After two weeks, adult butterflies emerge and exit the nest.

Butterfly-ant coevolution

1 **A female** *Niphanda fusca* butterfly cements a line of pale blue eggs onto the stalk of a plant where she has observed bustling black ants tending colonies of aphids.

2 **After hatching,** *Niphanda fusca* caterpillars seek out the aphids, upon which they feed. Normally, the ants would defend the aphids, which provide them with food.

4 **Ants feed** the caterpillars that have been deposited in their nest *(below)*. The caterpillars gain enormous safety from predators by living in the well-defended nest.

5 **When the** caterpillars have eaten, they secrete a sweet liquid, which in turn provides a favorite food for the ants.

3 **Instead of** killing the caterpillars, the ants allow them to grow to a given size, then carry them back to the nest, clutching them in their jaws, or mandibles.

79

How Do Insects Become Adults?

Nearly all insects go through a metamorphosis, changing shape one or more times before becoming adults. In complete metamorphosis insects hatch from eggs and become larvae. They soon outgrow their inflexible outer shells and go through a molt. In this process, the larva splits open and discards the old shell, exposing a soft new shell, which quickly hardens. Each time an insect molts, it enters a new stage, or instar, until finally it passes through a pupal stage, after which it emerges as an adult. Other insects go through a so-called incomplete metamorphosis, which proceeds from egg to immature form, or nymph, to adult.

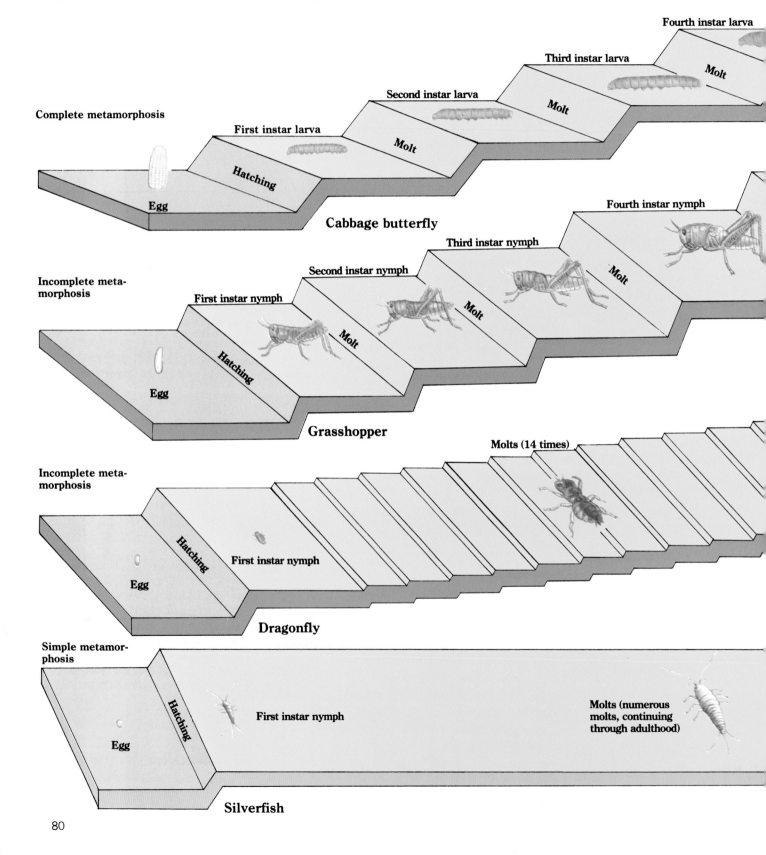

Complete metamorphosis

Egg — Hatching — First instar larva — Molt — Second instar larva — Molt — Third instar larva — Molt — Fourth instar larva — Molt

Cabbage butterfly

Incomplete metamorphosis

Egg — Hatching — First instar nymph — Molt — Second instar nymph — Molt — Third instar nymph — Molt — Fourth instar nymph

Grasshopper

Incomplete metamorphosis

Egg — Hatching — First instar nymph — Molts (14 times)

Dragonfly

Simple metamorphosis

Egg — Hatching — First instar nymph — Molts (numerous molts, continuing through adulthood)

Silverfish

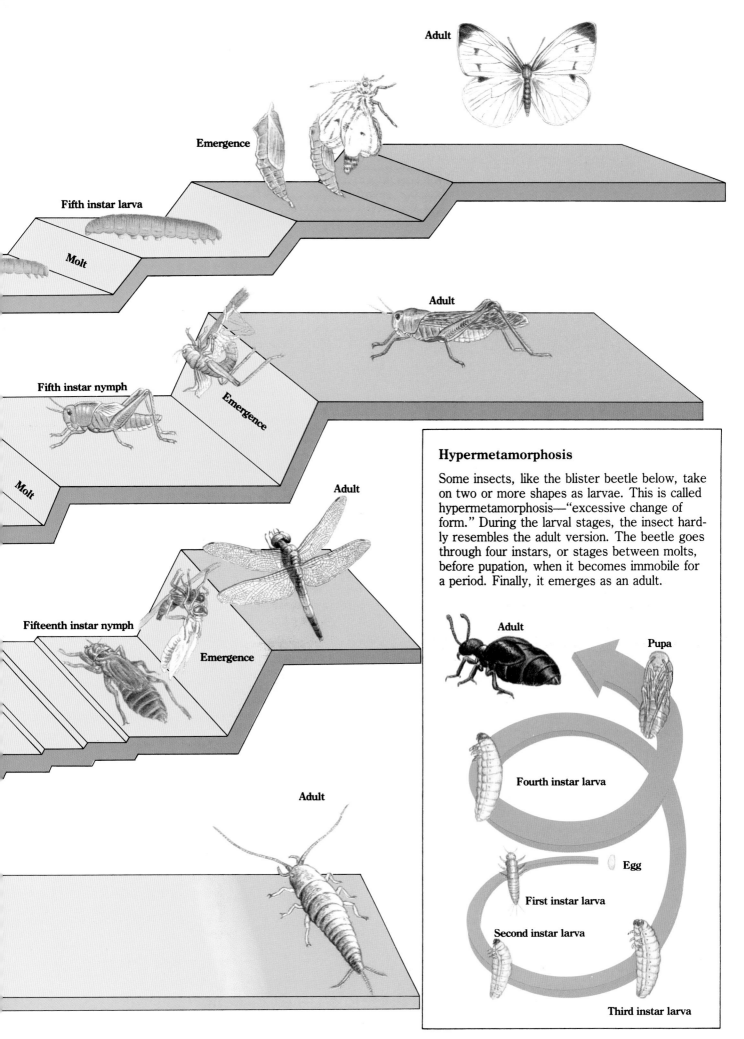

Adult

Emergence

Fifth instar larva

Molt

Adult

Fifth instar nymph

Emergence

Molt

Adult

Fifteenth instar nymph

Emergence

Adult

Hypermetamorphosis

Some insects, like the blister beetle below, take on two or more shapes as larvae. This is called hypermetamorphosis—"excessive change of form." During the larval stages, the insect hardly resembles the adult version. The beetle goes through four instars, or stages between molts, before pupation, when it becomes immobile for a period. Finally, it emerges as an adult.

Adult

Pupa

Fourth instar larva

Egg

First instar larva

Second instar larva

Third instar larva

What Is Pupation?

Among more evolutionarily advanced insects, the last phase of growth before adulthood is pupation. From the outside, pupae appear barely alive. During this stage they eat nothing at all, while their bodies are held immobile, swathed in a woven cocoon or barrel-shaped casing. But a profound transformation is taking place inside, as larvae literally rebuild themselves.

Pupation is triggered by increased production of hormones, or chemicals produced in the body, that are responsible for metamorphosis, and by a suppression of the so-called juvenile hormone, which abounds in the larval state. As a result, clusters of cells that have remained nearly inactive since hatching begin to grow and divide, forming the organs and structures of the adult insect, including antennae, wings, and legs. During pupation, a larva takes on the characteristic three-part body of the adult, made up of head, thorax, and abdomen. As illustrated at right and below, a larval caterpillar passes from the pupal state, in which it is covered by a protective chrysalis, to adulthood.

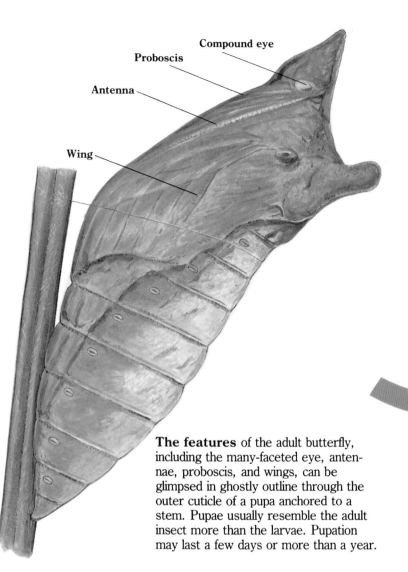

Compound eye
Proboscis
Antenna
Wing

The features of the adult butterfly, including the many-faceted eye, antennae, proboscis, and wings, can be glimpsed in ghostly outline through the outer cuticle of a pupa anchored to a stem. Pupae usually resemble the adult insect more than the larvae. Pupation may last a few days or more than a year.

Complete metamorphosis

The transformation of a crawling caterpillar into a monarch butterfly is one of nature's more splendid spectacles. Three hormones spur metamorphosis in butterflies. The first hormone produced in the brain causes the prothoracic gland to release a second hormone, which governs molts from the time that an egg hatches until it pupates. The third, the juvenile hormone, produced by an endocrine organ called the corpora allata, is present throughout the larval stage and absent during pupal to adult metamorphosis.

When a monarch caterpillar hatches, it begins to feed on poisonous milkweed, which will not harm it.

By the fifth molt, the caterpillar shows off warning colors that proclaim it poisonous to others.

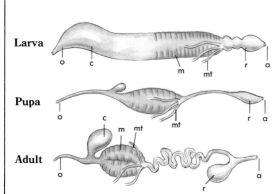

Digestive alterations

During pupation the digestive tract changes. The esophagus (o), crop (c), and midgut (m), designed for breaking down leaves, become narrow; the Malpighian tubules (mt) gain kinks, and the rectum (a) balloons to a rectal sac (r), all to get ready for an adult diet of nectar and sap.

Cells make a wing mosaic

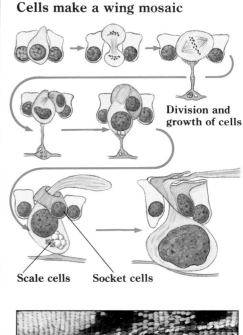

Division and growth of cells

Scale cells   Socket cells

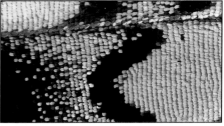

Pigmented scales dot a swallowtail wing.

The pattern on a butterfly's wings is produced by individually pigmented scales, shown in the photographic enlargement above. During pupation, clusters of epidermal cells divide and rearrange themselves *(top)*. Some die, others take the shape of sockets that hold greatly enlarged scale cells in place.

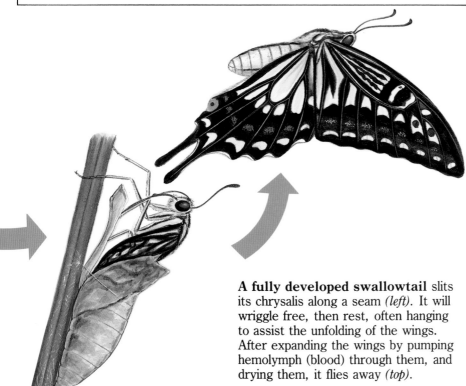

A fully developed swallowtail slits its chrysalis along a seam *(left)*. It will wriggle free, then rest, often hanging to assist the unfolding of the wings. After expanding the wings by pumping hemolymph (blood) through them, and drying them, it flies away *(top)*.

Before its final molt, the caterpillar fastens itself to a leaf to hang upside down. When the skin splits, a smooth, legless chrysalis emerges.

As a pupa, the monarch rearranges its tissues. The legs along the abdomen wither; the legs of the thorax grow longer. Mouth parts change to nectar feeders and wings grow.

In the final step, a young monarch pushes out of its shell, pumps blood into its wings, and after a brief rest to let the wings dry, takes flight.

Can All Insects Fly?

The development of wings in insects was a major evolutionary step. Today most insects do have wings, but there are exceptions. Some species of insects have wings that do not function or that wither away during the course of adulthood. Others emerge from the pupal state entirely without wings.

Wings originally evolved as lateral extensions of the thorax that permitted the insect to glide. Later the flight muscle machinery evolved, then the ability to twist and fold the wings over the body. Further evolution has meant that insects for whom flight is unimportant have lost their wings altogether or carried only a rudimentary version of them into adulthood. On these pages are some examples of insects (not shown to scale) that can only crawl or seldom take to the air.

Less than a half-inch long, primitive silverfish *(Lepisma saccharina)* have no wings. They feed on starch in books, paper, and fabrics.

Bloodsucking fleas, of the order Siphonaptera, lack wings but have powerful legs that allow them to travel by great leaps.

Scavenging earwigs, of the order Dermaptera, usually have no wings, but a few species have two or four short and leathery wings.

A parasite, the sucking louse has no wings. These lice feed on blood from mammals and birds, piercing a victim's skin with their pointed stylets.

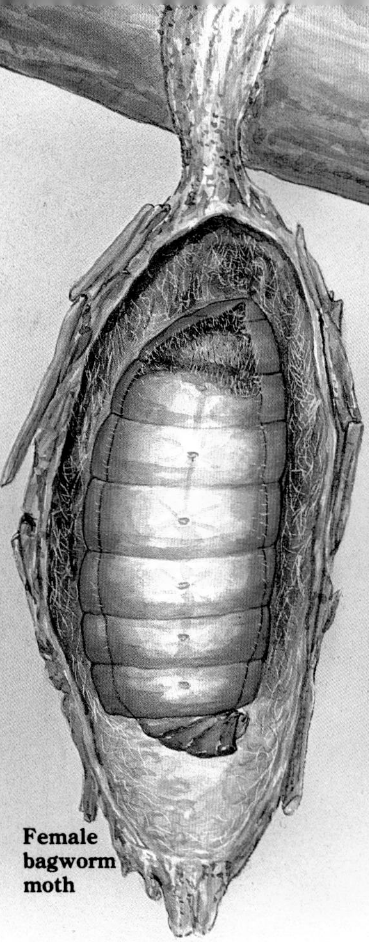

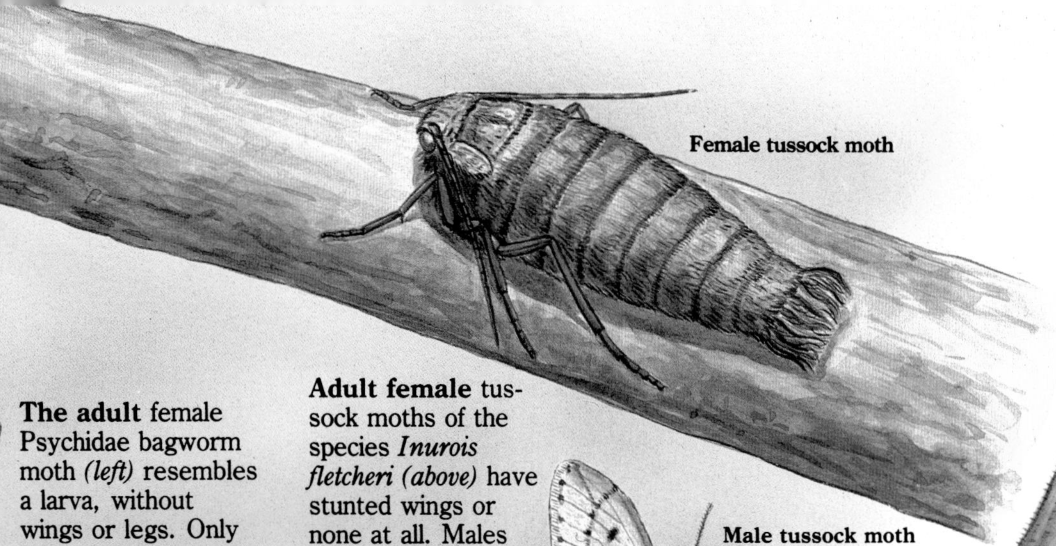

Female tussock moth

The adult female Psychidae bagworm moth *(left)* resembles a larva, without wings or legs. Only males take wing, as below, to find mates.

Adult female tussock moths of the species *Inurois fletcheri (above)* have stunted wings or none at all. Males *(right)* sport wings.

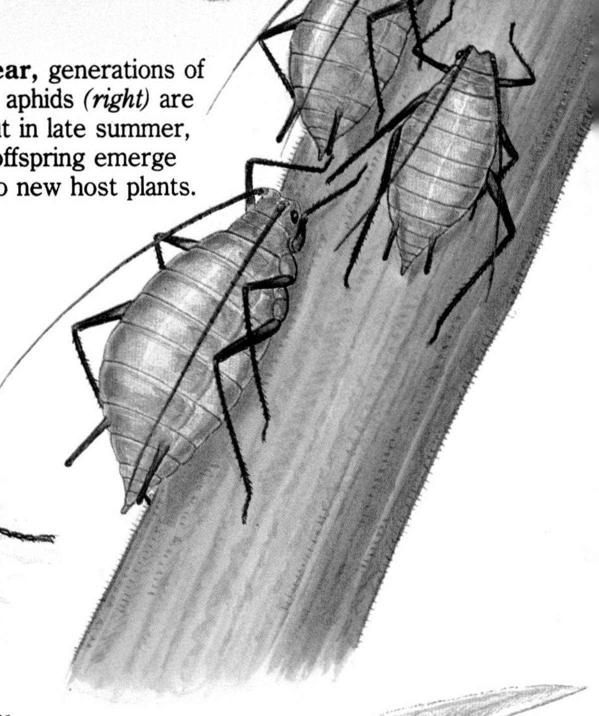

Male tussock moth

Male bagworm moth

Female bagworm moth

Each year, generations of wingless aphids *(right)* are born. But in late summer, winged offspring emerge and fly to new host plants.

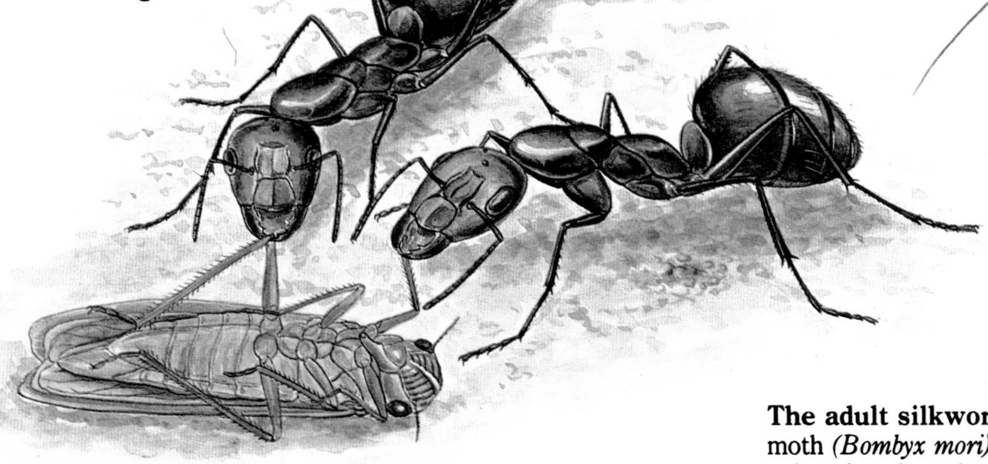

The worker castes of most species of ant are wingless; only the queens have wings.

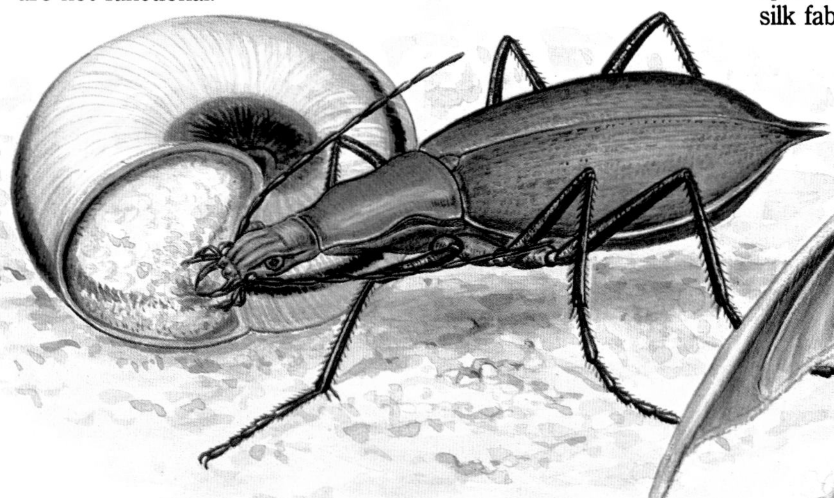

The adult silkworm moth *(Bombyx mori)* lives only a few days, laying eggs and flying rarely. Larvae spin threads used to make silk fabric.

The beetle *Damaster blaptoides* eats land snails. Its forewings, held close to the body, are not functional.

85

Why Do Locusts Swarm?

Locusts—migratory grasshoppers of the Acrididae family—go through two phases in their adult lives, one solitary, the other gregarious. Feeding alone, a locust in the solitary phase is yellowish and has long hind legs and a pronounced thoracic shield behind its head. Under normal circumstances, locusts mate and lay eggs in the same breeding ground year after year. When the population becomes too crowded, however, a pheromone released in the insects' droppings makes the locusts secrete some hormones that cause their bodies to change. The cuticle darkens, the hind legs and thoracic shield shrink, and the wings lengthen. Taking to the air in swarms, the locusts migrate to new territory.

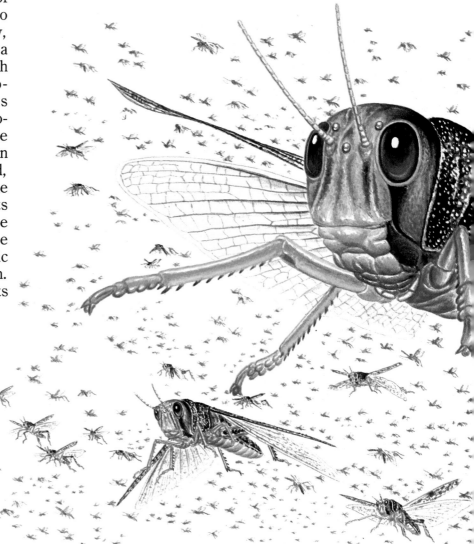

Subtle shifts in color and form

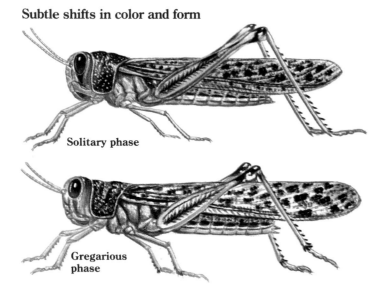

Solitary phase

Gregarious phase

A locust in the solitary phase *(top)* is well equipped for jumping, while the darker gregarious, or migratory, locust *(above)* has features that suit it for long flights.

Swarming behavior

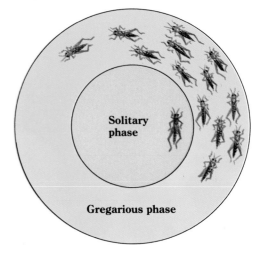

Solitary phase

Gregarious phase

A solitary-phase locust in a cage *(center)* encircled by locusts in the gregarious phase *(outer ring)* soon takes on the characteristics of the group.

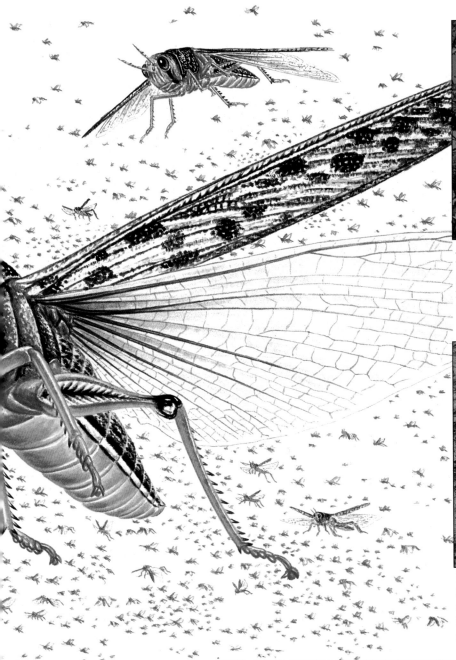

A horde of locusts devours a bush, undeterred by its thorns. Corn, millet, and other grains can be stripped to the ground by the insects. Only a few plants, like the Indian chinaberry tree, resist their onslaught.

Locusts on the march are a daunting menace to farmers. When these ravenous insects descend on the countryside, they devastate the crops in the fields, often causing famine.

Mass migration

In 1985 heavy rains following a prolonged drought in west-central Africa spurred an explosion of locusts. Swarming northwest from Sudan and Ethiopia, the insects devoured crops in their path, reaching the continent's west coast in 1988. From there, portions of the original band fanned north to the Mediterranean Sea and Italy while others spanned the Atlantic, carried toward the Caribbean by easterly winds. A fraction of the swarm, embarking from Senegal and Mauritania, battled contrary winds and reached the tiny island of Barbados, after a 3,000-mile flight. Routes are indicated by pink arrows in the map at right.

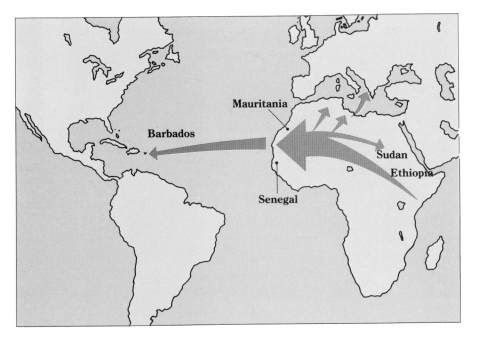

What Causes Insect Outbreaks?

Insect outbreaks—sudden explosions of insect populations that result in damage to crops and other plants—have a number of natural and man-made causes. Temperatures or moisture levels that are abnormally high or low, stresses that affect the chemical balance of plants, and even the spraying of pesticides can trigger such outbreaks, which in the past were known as plagues. In the case of the webworm, shown at right, cool spring weather often leads to outbreaks. Because ants that normally prey on webworm larvae eat fewer of them when temperatures are lower, a greater-than-usual number of larvae make it to adulthood. Among brown planthoppers *(below)*, reproduction actually increases after certain types of insecticides are sprayed on fields because their natural enemies are killed in the process.

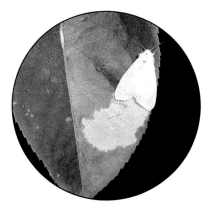

A female tiger moth (*Hyphantria cunea*) lays eggs on a cherry leaf *(above)*. In late summer and fall, larvae will hatch.

Tiger moth larvae, called fall webworms, feed on leaves *(near right),* then spin gauzy enclosures on tree limbs *(far right)* and continue to feed.

Planthopper explosions

The brown planthopper *(Nilaparvata lugens)* feeds on rice plants and poses a major threat to food supplies in Asia. During the rainy monsoon season, the insects migrate northeastward from winter feeding grounds in Southeast Asia, maturing along the way. Arriving in Japan, they produce one or two short-winged generations; then in the fall, they begin feasting on rice fields. In some years their population increases 200-fold, greatly damaging rice crops.

Periodical cicada cycles

In the eastern United States, cicadas go through either 13- or 17-year life cycles. Most of a cicada's life is spent as a nymph, feeding underground and molting. Only during the last month or so does a nymph emerge from the soil, go through a final molt to adult form, and mate *(right)*. Scientists have identified dozens of broods of each type of cicada that follow their own 13- or 17-year calendars. Some broods are especially large, and the years during which their members reach maturity are hard on the environment. The females lay eggs inside tree twigs in nurseries and orchards *(inset, right)*, severely damaging young trees.

What Is Biological Pest Control?

After World War II, chemicals were thought to be the ultimate weapon against crop-damaging insects. Ecologists now recognize, however, that pesticides may worsen agricultural problems. Pesticides sometimes prompt the evolution of strains of insects that can survive even the most toxic sprays. Because pesticides pollute soils and waterways and enter the food chain, possibly harming the health of animals and humans, scientists have sought safer ways of defeating pests. Biological pest control draws on an understanding of natural enemies among insects. By introducing known predators of certain pests into fields or orchards, as shown below, farmers can reduce the populations of these pests in a natural way and keep crop damage to a minimum.

Scale

Parasitic wasp

Cottony
cushion
scale

Red scale

Aphytis wasp

Ladybug

The scale insect *Unasipis yanonensis (far left)* feeds on citrus fruit, sucking the sap from leaves, stems, and fruit. Such infestation causes the trees to wilt and the fruit to spoil. But since the introduction in 1980 of two species of parasitic wasps of the Encyrtidae family, the pest is losing the battle, making one case of successful biological pest control.

Cottony cushion scale *(Icerya purchasi)* lays its eggs on citrus and other fruit trees. But the pest has an enemy in the ladybug *(Vedalia cardinalis)* from Australia, which feeds on the scale. Since the 1800s, many groves throughout the United States, as well as Asia, have been saved from complete ruin by introduction of this beneficial predator.

In California, red scales are the most damaging pests to feed on citrus fruit. When hatched from the eggs, nymphs settle in one spot to feed and secrete a waxy covering over their bodies. Males fertilize the immobile females, who give birth to two or three young every day for several months. But the parasitic wasp *Aphytis* attacks this pest and keeps its spread under control.

4
Insect and Spider Nests

A spider's web, stretching across a basement corner or between two twigs, is a familiar sight. So, too, are wasp nests and anthills. But these are only among the most obvious ways that spiders and insects build their nests. Water spiders, for instance, build their homes underwater, spinning silken tents that they fill with bubbles of air. Ground bees, as their name suggests, dig long tunnels into the ground with many side rooms. Some species of ants build complex underground cities, and leaf-rolling weevils make their nests in

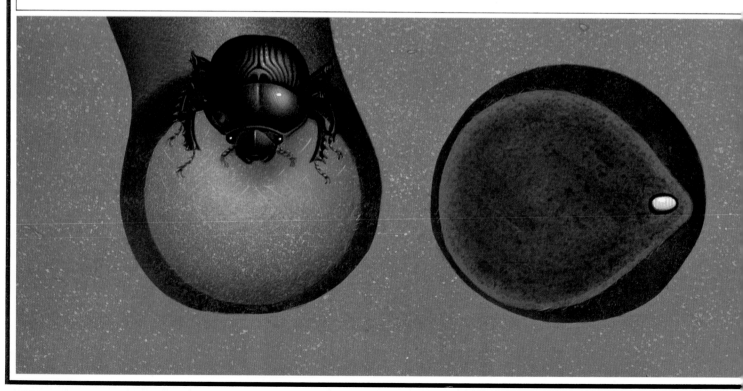

trees by winding leaves into structures that look like green egg rolls.

In most cases, insect and spider nests are a safe place in which the female of the species can deposit her eggs, together with a supply of food for the hungry hatchlings. The dung beetle larva begins its life sealed inside a ball of dung that has been rolled into a burrow. The larva eats from the ball as it grows, and when it reaches adulthood, it makes its way to the surface. Some newborn insects, however, have to build their own nests. The bagworm moth larva covers itself with bits of food that it collects soon after emerging from its egg. The spittlebug nymph makes its protective nest out of bubbles that it blows around itself using plant juice.

Social hunting wasps build hanging cities *(above)*, while the dung beetle *(bottom)* digs a simple hole for its nest. Whether in the air or underground, both types of nest are secure places in which a larva can hatch from an egg, have a ready food supply, and grow into an adult.

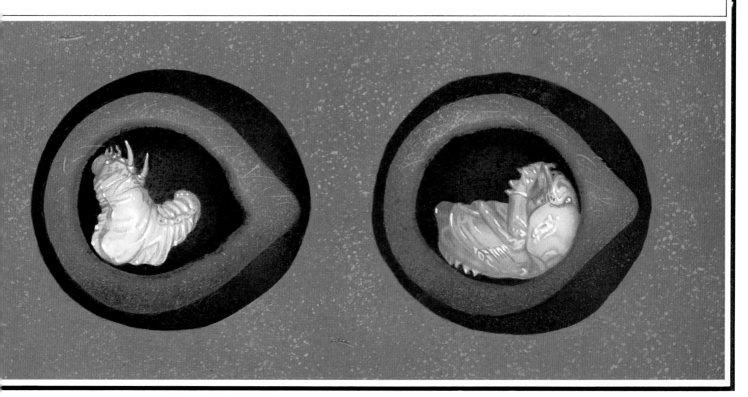

How Do Spiders Spin Their Threads?

All spiders produce silk threads from spinnerets on their abdomens. Spiders use silk to catch and bind prey, to build webs and cocoons, and to spin draglines. Each use needs a different kind of silk, for which some spiders have up to six types of silk glands. These glands produce liquid silk, which moves through a duct to a microscopic spigot on one of six spinnerets. The liquid turns to thread when it squirts from the spinneret.

The female golden web spider wraps its eggs in a silken cocoon. This silk comes from the tubuliformes gland, located in the spider's abdomen with five other types of silk glands.

Spinnerets
Aciniformes gland
Tubuliformes gland
Midgut

Uses of thread

Dragline. When walking, many spiders pull a dragline that serves as a lifeline, should they have to jump clear of danger. This silk is twice as elastic as nylon.

Nests. The funnel weaver waits for prey in its tunnel-shaped nest. A purse web spider spends its life in a sealed, silken tube, spearing its prey through the web.

Webs. The orb web consists of three structural elements: the central hub, the radial threads, and the sticky outer spiral.

The spinneret. Most spiders have three pairs of spinnerets. Each pair is fed by several silk glands. Spinnerets are muscular and release thread independently of one another.

The cribellum. Some spiders have an additional spinneret with over 40,000 spigots. Each produces a very fine thread that combines with the others in a silk band, used to catch prey.

The spigots. Each of the many spigots on a spinneret is fed by its own silk gland, emitting threads of different thickness *(dark tips)*.

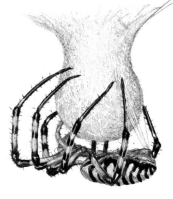

Cocoons. A female spider produces more thread in spinning a cocoon for her eggs than she does for any other purpose.

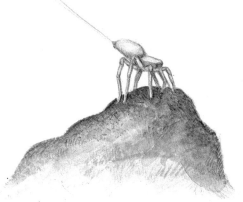

Flight thread. A newly hatched spider leaves its cocoon by using a silk thread to catch the wind.

Swathing band. A spider saves its prey for a later meal by wrapping it in hundreds of thin threads from the aciniformes gland.

What Is a Water Spider's Nest Like?

Of the 30,000 species of spiders in the world, only the water spider swims, hunts, mates, and builds its nest underwater. This spider cannot actually breathe underwater like a fish; instead, it lives in an air bubble trapped under a silk canopy, much like a diving bell. The spider's genus name, *Argyros,* comes from the Greek for "silver," because the air bubble shines with a silvery hue through the water. The spider also raises young in the air bubble. When the spider ventures out of its nest to hunt, it carries a bubble on its abdomen from which it can get oxygen as needed.

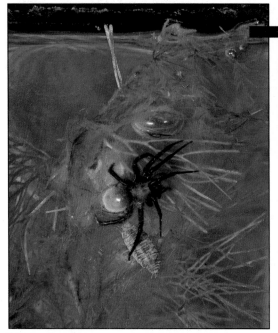

A water spider anchors its nest to water plants.

Building an underwater nest

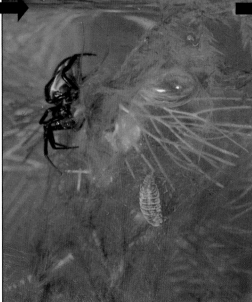

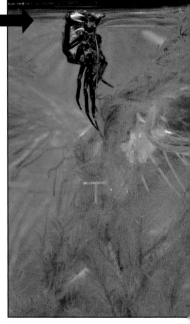

With its bubble of air, a water spider looks for a suitable clump of weeds to build its nest. It begins by weaving the nest's ceiling.

The water spider carries air bubbles from the surface to the silk patch. As the air pocket grows, the spider extends the dome.

At the surface, the spider traps air between its abdomen and hind legs.

During the day, the water spider sits in its nest with its front legs sticking into the water. There, it waits for a water insect to pass by. The spider then pounces quickly, killing its prey and drawing it into its nest.

The spider makes six or more quick trips to the surface to fill its nest with air. Oxygen and carbon dioxide levels remain even because the spider replenishes the store with fresh supplies.

Life of a water spider

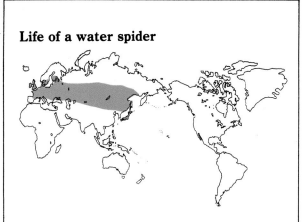

Distribution. Water spiders are found throughout temperate Asia and Europe, including Great Britain and Ireland. They live in lakes, ponds, and ditches.

Predation. Water spiders always feed in their underwater nests. At night, the spider may leave its nest and swim in search of food, but it returns with its captured meal to the air bubble.

Reproduction. Water spiders mate in the female's nest. The female then builds a silk egg sac and lays 50 to 100 eggs. The young emerge three to four weeks later. They leave the nest covered with bubbles trapped by hydrophobic hair on their abdomens.

Why Do Ants Protect Certain Plants?

Many ants and plants have evolved so that their survival depends on one another. These relationships, called symbiosis, take several forms. The plant may provide the ant with a secure place to build a nest, while the ant may fend off the plant's predators. In some cases, a plant produces food and nectar for its ant colony, or the ants provide nutrients for their host plant. Ants may also distribute a plant's seeds, pollinate its flowers, or even chop down its competitors growing nearby. One ant species will attack and destroy any plant growing within 15 inches of its home plant.

Ant and plant symbiosis

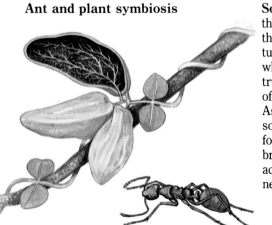

Hypoclinea ant

Some ants build their nests around the winding structures of epiphytes, which grow from trunks and branches of trees throughout Asia. The plants absorb nutrients from food and organic debris that the ants accumulate in their nests.

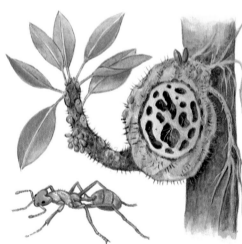

Irdomyrmex ant

An ant plant develops a large, honeycombed structure where its roots grow into the bark of the tree upon which it lives. One of several ant species will bore a hole into the tuber and build its nest in the chambers there. The ant plant absorbs nutrients from waste material carried into some of these chambers.

Aztec ants of Central and South America *(below)* repel insects that damage the trumpet tree, on which they live. In return for this protection, the plant provides the ants with both a home and a food supply. The ants nest in the soft, hollow stems of the trees, but the nest does not seem to harm the tree.

An Aztec ant feeds on tiny food bodies. These structures grow on the pad of tissue that develops beneath each leaf junction. The trumpet tree produces the food bodies specifically to attract ants, which help it to thrive.

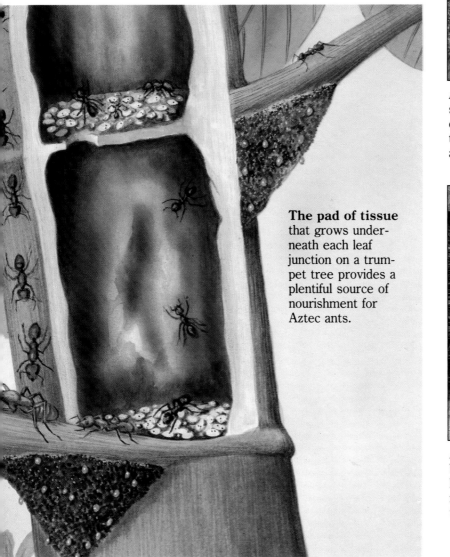

The pad of tissue that grows underneath each leaf junction on a trumpet tree provides a plentiful source of nourishment for Aztec ants.

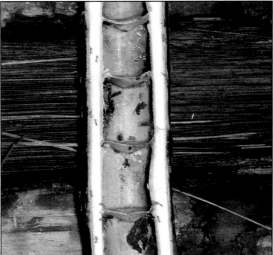

A queen Aztec ant cuts her way into a hollow between knots in a growing trumpet tree and lays her eggs there. Afterward, the ant will mate again, make a hole into the next section of the tree, and lay a new batch of eggs.

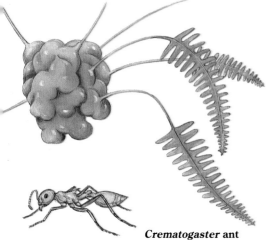

Ants in Central and South America may carry seeds into their nests, and some of these seeds sprout. The plants growing in these ant gardens get nutrients from food and debris in the nest. The ants eat the fruit and nectar that the plants produce.

Crematogaster **ant**

Pseudomyrmex **ant**

The bull-horn acacia plant has hollow thorns where *Pseudomyrmex* ants nest. The plant also feeds the ants nectar. In return, the ants use their stingers to keep the acacia free of plant-eating insects and mammals. Even brushing an acacia provokes its ants to swarm and sting the unlucky passerby.

Who Builds Bubble Nests?

From spring through early summer, clumps of bubbles appear on the branches of trees and shrubs. Hiding beneath these bubbles are tiny wingless insects, the nymphs of spittlebugs. As soon as they hatch, the nymphs begin feeding themselves by sucking juice from the plant they live on. After digesting the juice and absorbing the nutrients, the nymphs add a detergent-like material and excrete bubbles. The moist bubbles may protect the delicate nymphs from drying out as they develop. The bubbles may also taste bad, which would discourage predators from digging through them to get to the nymph.

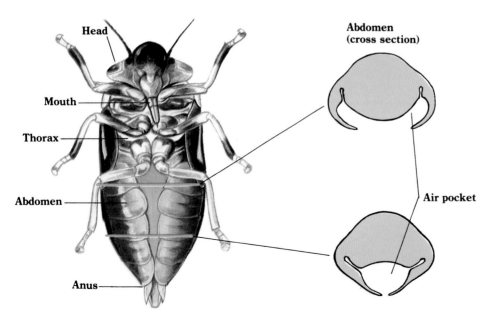

An adult white-banded spittlebug can use its wings to escape from predators, find food, and search for a mate.

Making bubbles

As a spittlebug nymph stands head down and draws juice from a plant stem, it produces soaplike bubbles from its anus. These sticky bubbles gradually surround the brightly colored nymph and provide a protective covering.

Spittlebug nymph

The abdomen of the spittlebug nymph curls downward to form an air pocket *(left, bottom)*. The insect breathes through this pocket. Some of the air mixes with spittle as it emerges from the nymph's anus, producing the protective froth. The bubbles build up from the nymph's rear end until they cover its topside. A nymph can make a large amount of foam quickly. If other nymphs are nearby, their bubbles can overlap, forming a larger nest that contains several ⅛-inch-long nymphs.

Head

Mouth

Thorax

Abdomen

Anus

Abdomen (cross section)

Air pocket

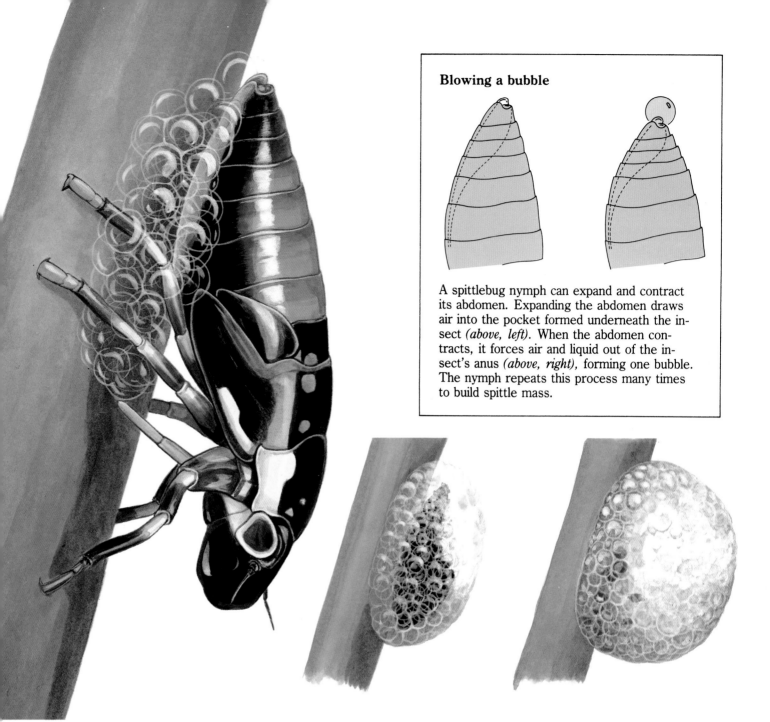

Blowing a bubble

A spittlebug nymph can expand and contract its abdomen. Expanding the abdomen draws air into the pocket formed underneath the insect *(above, left)*. When the abdomen contracts, it forces air and liquid out of the insect's anus *(above, right)*, forming one bubble. The nymph repeats this process many times to build spittle mass.

Feeding

The spittlebug nymph feeds on a plant's juices through its stylet, a hollow, needlelike probe that the insect projects from its mouth *(right)*. After hatching, the nymph inserts its stylet into the plant stem on which it was born. The stylet is long enough to reach the vessels that carry sap through the plant. Once it has tapped into this plentiful food source, the nymph sucks the sap through a microscopically thin tube inside the stylet. Sap is largely water, but it does contain all the nutrients that the nymph needs in order to grow to adulthood. After the sap passes through the nymph's digestive system, it leaves the insect's body at the anus. There, the juices become foam.

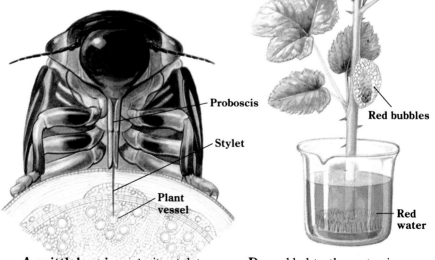

Proboscis

Stylet

Plant vessel

Red bubbles

Red water

A spittlebug inserts its stylet into a sap-carrying vein of its home plant.

Dye added to the water in which a plant grows shows up in the spittlebug's bubbles.

What Is a Bagworm's Nest?

Bagworm moths are hardly ever seen. The females never leave their nests, and the males are alive for only a short time. It's the caterpillars of the bagworm moth and their distinctive nests, hanging like tiny bags from tree branches, that give these insects away.

Depending on the species, a bagworm eats leaves, evergreen needles, and other vegetation. As it eats, it ties some of this plant material around itself with silk to form a bag. In spring and summer, the bag helps the caterpillar conserve water and fend off predators as it moves around in search of food. The caterpillar enlarges its bag as it grows and sheds its skin, forcing the skin through a hole in the bottom of the bag. As the caterpillar matures, it attaches its bag to a twig with silk. Then it slips inside and seals the bag. Over the next few weeks, the caterpillar goes through the pupa stage to become an adult moth. If the resulting moth is a male, it emerges from its bag, unfurls its wings and antennae, and flies off in search of a mate. A female bagworm moth lacks wings and remains in its bag awaiting a mate. After mating it lays its eggs in the bottom of the bag on top of the last piece of shed skin. The female then crawls from the bag, seals it tight for winter, and dies.

The nest. A bagworm caterpillar makes its nest from leaves and small twigs cut from the tree on which it lives. Silk binds the plant material together and forms a weathertight seal that protects the caterpillar as it grows. When the caterpillar reaches maturity, it attaches its nest to a twig.

A variety of bagworm nests

Each bagworm species makes a bag nest of unique size and structure. The bag's shape and composition depend largely on the type of food that the caterpillar eats and what other building supplies are at hand. An African bagworm, for example, uses the sharp thorns of the acacia plant. The Abbott's bagworm and evergreen bagworm have similar diets, but the Abbott's bagworm covers its bag with twigs that it places horizontally, while the evergreen bagworm attaches the sticks vertically.

Black-winged dwarf bagworm. This species uses silk, but no plant material, to make its bag.

Mahasena bagworm. Shed skin lines the opening of this bag. Broken leaves lie beneath the skin.

Young bagworm caterpillars build their nests right on their backs. They carry the bags around with them as they search for food to eat.

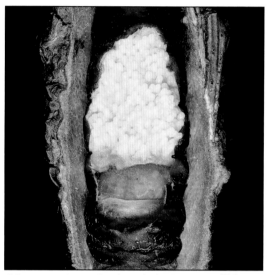

After mating, the female bagworm will lay some 3,000 to 4,000 eggs in its bag. These will hatch in spring.

A mature bagworm caterpillar has sealed itself into its bag. The caterpillar will now begin its metamorphosis, the process in which it turns from a caterpillar into a moth.

Psyche bagworm. Dead leaves from rice plants make up this bagworm's nest.

Psyche niphonica. This species fixes its nest to a tree trunk covered with lichen, its favorite food.

***Euploca* bagworm.** Sand covers this species' nest. It lives on stone walls or rocks covered with lichen.

How Does a Leaf Roller Make a Nest?

In forests, vineyards, and orchards throughout the world hang small green objects that look like cigars or egg rolls. They are the work of leaf-rolling weevils, small beetles that deposit their eggs inside rolled-up leaves. The females of many species of weevil roll leaves in a certain way after cutting the leaf in precise spots to make the job easier. The tightly rolled leaves provide both a safe place for the eggs to develop and a ready source of food when the weevils hatch. Some species place many eggs in a roll, while others create a nest for only one egg.

1 A common leaf-roller female starts by cutting a notch on one side of a beech leaf.

2 The leaf roller makes the same cut on the opposite side, stopping at the center.

3 The leaf wilts in a few minutes, allowing the weevil to begin the rolling process.

7 The weevil bites the leaf to make winding easier. Its left legs pull the leaf toward its body; its right legs wind the leaf into a roll.

8 Using its legs on one side, the weevil starts to cover the end of the roll.

9 The weevil completes the nest by tucking the final piece in place.

4 The weevil walks the length of the leaf, pressing the two halves together.

5 Winding begins at the tip. The weevil uses its legs to pull the leaf toward its body.

6 The weevil makes a slit and lays an egg inside, then winds the leaf further and seals it.

Other leaf-roller nests

Leaf-rolling weevils show a variety of techniques for building their nests. Some cut leaves in such a way that the leaves roll themselves into the proper shape. Others use vines to tie the roll together. Certain species secrete a glue that they use to keep the nest from unwinding.

10 The finished nest *(right)* is tightly rolled and sealed. The same nest cut in half *(below)* reveals a single egg inside. When the larva hatches from the egg, it eats its way through the many layers of the leaf.

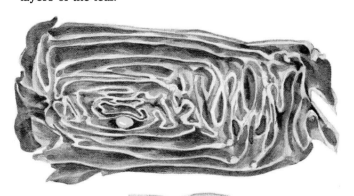

11 The weevil moves to a new leaf to start another nest.

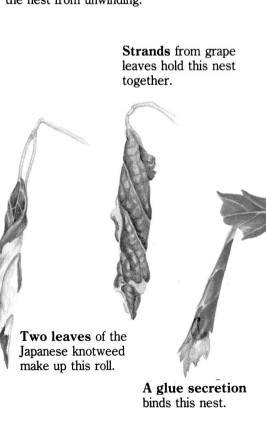

Strands from grape leaves hold this nest together.

Two leaves of the Japanese knotweed make up this roll.

A glue secretion binds this nest.

Why Does a Dung Beetle Roll Manure?

One large group of insects plays an unusual role in keeping the Earth clean. These are the dung beetles, which not only eat the dung left behind by plant-eating animals but also use it as a nursery for their young by laying eggs in small dung balls. The dung beetles, which include the sacred scarab of Egypt, break off pieces of dung, shape them into balls, and roll them to their nests. Some species may roll their dung balls more than 100 yards.

Dung beetles roll dung away because competition for this nutritious material is intense. In fact, fierce battles often erupt. To defend its prize, the beetle holding a dung ball will climb onto it and grasp it with its four hind legs. It uses its front legs to repel attackers, flipping them off as they try to climb up the ball.

An African dung beetle cuts a piece of elephant dung. It uses its head and forelegs to tamp the piece into a ball. The beetle uses its hind legs to hold on to its harvest to prevent another beetle from stealing it.

Pushing with its powerful legs, the dung beetle rolls its dung ball to its nest.

A dung beetle nest

Dung beetles use dung in a variety of ways. Some lay their eggs directly in the large dung pile. Others build underground nests with an elaborate system of tunnels. Then they roll dung balls to the nest, dropping smaller pieces into the tunnels. The beetles store part of their harvest for their own meals, while the female uses the rest to lay her eggs inside. Certain species pile all the egg-containing dung balls in one tunnel, while other species spread their eggs throughout the nest. Some dung beetles coat their egg-containing balls with mud.

When it finds a good spot, the beetle digs a hole under the dung ball. In some instances, this hole may be a foot deep or more.

3

The female beetle molds the dung ball into shape *(right),* lays one egg in the tip, and covers it with mud.

4

The cutaway of a dung ball *(below)* shows the egg's location and the protective mud.

Dung

Egg

Mud

Dung and mud

Development of a dung beetle

After the dung beetle larva hatches from the egg, it eats its way to the center of the ball of dung. The larva knows instinctively which direction to turn within its dark chamber.

The larva grows to its final stage inside the mud-encrusted chamber. As it consumes the dung, the beetle larva smears its own droppings along the inside wall, thereby strengthening the chamber.

Once the larva matures into an adult dung beetle, it bites through the hard chamber and breaks apart the dung ball. The beetle then crawls to the surface and goes in search of its own first dung pile.

Where Does the Ground Bee Live?

The simplest ground bee nest consists of one tunnel and one egg chamber *(left)*. Such nests are uncommon, probably because it takes so much effort to make the entrance tunnel and so little to make egg chambers.

Some ground bees build long side tunnels composed of several egg chambers. Each chamber contains one egg and is sealed off from neighboring chambers.

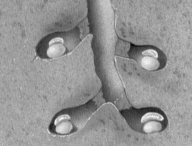

The long-waisted ground bee has a deep central tunnel with many egg chambers branching from it. Each chamber contains one egg or larva and a food ball.

As the larva grows, it devours the food ball left by its mother.

The tiny ground bee, a mere 0.2 to 0.4 inch long, is an excellent digger, capable of burrowing deep into the ground to make its nest. The female bee uses her powerful jaws, or mandibles, as a pickax and her claw feet as rakes to excavate a central tunnel and one or more chambers in which she lays her eggs.

The ground bee prepares her nest in early spring. She then forages among flowers for pollen, a rich source of protein, and nectar, a source of sugar. She returns to the nest to unload her harvest and then goes off after more pollen and nectar. After gathering a supply of food, the female combines the pollen with the nectar, shaping the mixture into food balls. The bee places one food ball in each egg chamber, lays a single egg on each ball, and seals the chamber. When the larva hatches, a ready supply of food will await it. When the larva grows into an adult bee, it emerges from its birth chamber.

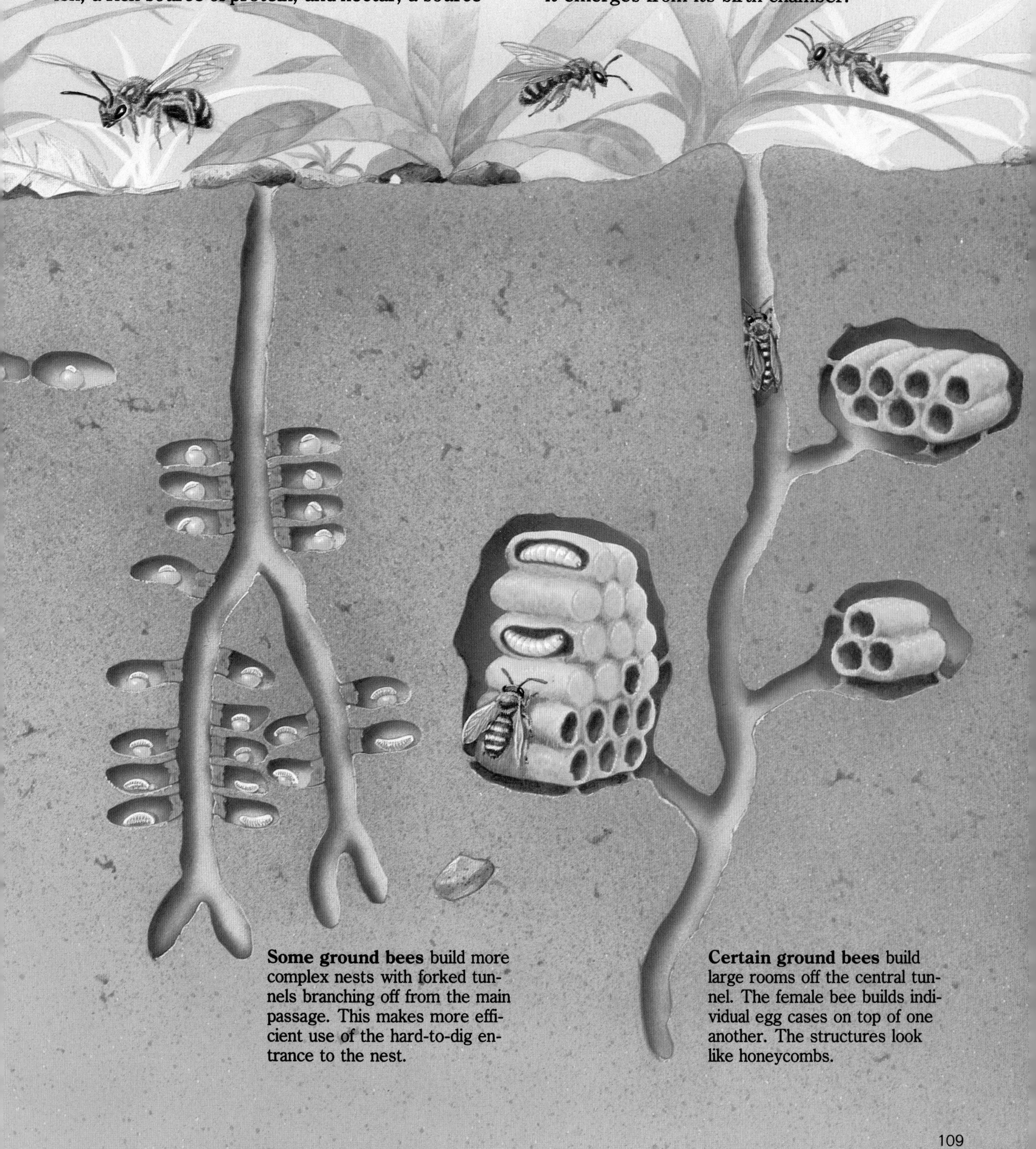

Some ground bees build more complex nests with forked tunnels branching off from the main passage. This makes more efficient use of the hard-to-dig entrance to the nest.

Certain ground bees build large rooms off the central tunnel. The female bee builds individual egg cases on top of one another. The structures look like honeycombs.

109

How Do Hunting Wasps Build Nests?

Of all the insects, hunting wasps may have evolved the widest range of talent for building nests. Some species of hunting wasps have few nest-building skills. They use their prey's underground nests instead to lay their eggs. Others dig their own holes, usually simple tunnels into which they will drag their prey and where they lay eggs.

But the social hunting wasps build elaborate nests made of mud or paper. Such a nest, hanging from a tree or under the eaves of a house, may contain hundreds of egg chambers that are arranged in multiple layers within the nest. Some of these nests can grow to as much as 3 feet in diameter and last as long as 25 years.

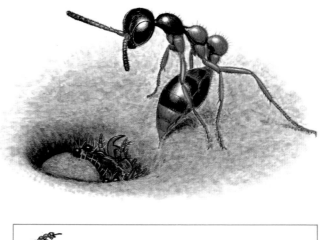

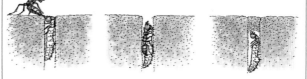

A female hunting wasp lures a tiger beetle larva from its hole *(above)*, paralyzes the larva with its sting, and lays an egg on top. The wasp pushes the larva back into its hole, where it will feed the developing wasp. This is the most primitive wasp nest.

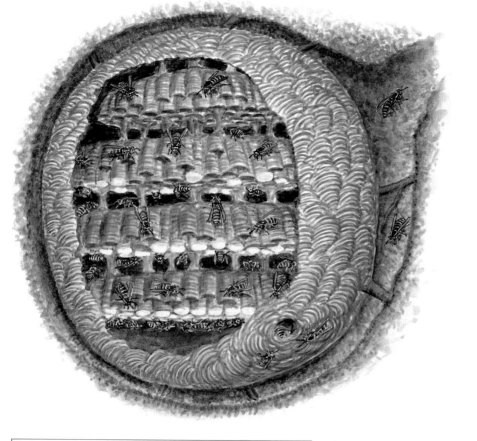

A yellow jacket nest resembles an apartment house made of paper. These social wasps expand their nest by removing the covering and adding new layers *(left)*.

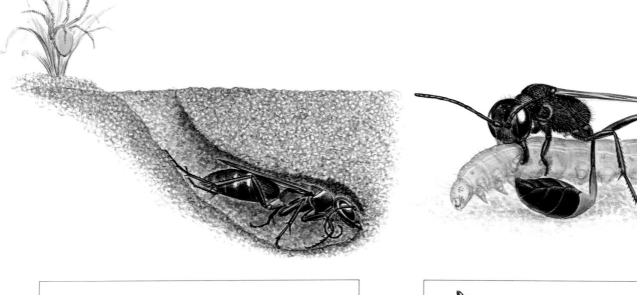

The tortoise shell wasp hunts spiders. The wasp hangs its prey from a blade of grass while it digs its nest hole. There it lays a single egg, brings in the dead spider for its larva to feed on, and seals the nest.

Some hunting wasps dig their underground nests before hunting for food. The female then fills the hole with one large caterpillar or several smaller insects before laying her egg.

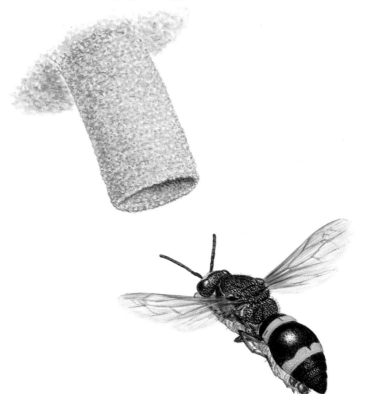

Paper wasp workers use their powerful jaws to rip fibers off pieces of wood. Their saliva softens the fibers, turning them into a papier-mâché-like material that makes the nest's thin but sturdy walls. The queen then lays one egg in each egg cell. When the eggs hatch, workers feed the larvae.

Grasping prey, a wasp returns to its mud nest. Having built a room, she lays an egg, then brings in the prey. When the room is filled, she builds a divider and starts again.

5

A Diversity of Defenses

To protect themselves from the host of enemies that threaten their struggle for existence, insects have evolved a variety of defenses. One of the most basic means of self-preservation is to flee from danger, a tactic mastered by the housefly, which swiftly takes flight. Some other insects attempt to elude predators by dropping suddenly from a resting place or freezing in a position that makes them appear to be a small twig or some other natural object.

Hiding from the enemy is also a common defensive pose. Many insects thrive in concealed

places, such as in tree trunks, under rocks, or underground. Others are disguised by camouflage, also called cryptic coloration, which enables them to blend into their background. Indeed, camouflage conceals so effectively that humans have borrowed the ploy.

To scare off would-be predators, certain insects flash special markings known as eyespots. Some have taken on the look of dangerous creatures, resembling snakes or scorpions, for example, to ward off assailants. And many species are truly armed for defense, relying on such effective

weapons as razor-sharp mandibles, venomous stingers, or poisonous gas to fight their enemies. This chapter takes a closer look at the defensive techniques, both passive and active, employed by many insects.

The striking colors of the poisonous yellow jacket, stink bug, ladybug pupa, and moth larva *(above, left to right)* remind predators that these insects are not safe to eat. Scary eyespots protect the planthopper, atlas moth, and silkworm larva *(below, left to right)*.

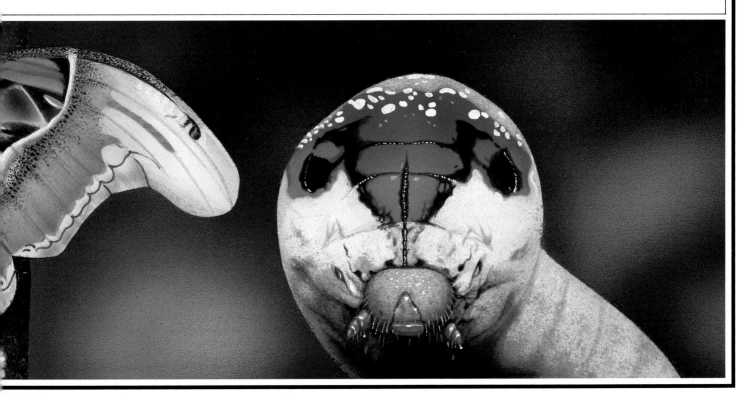

Who Are Insects' Natural Enemies?

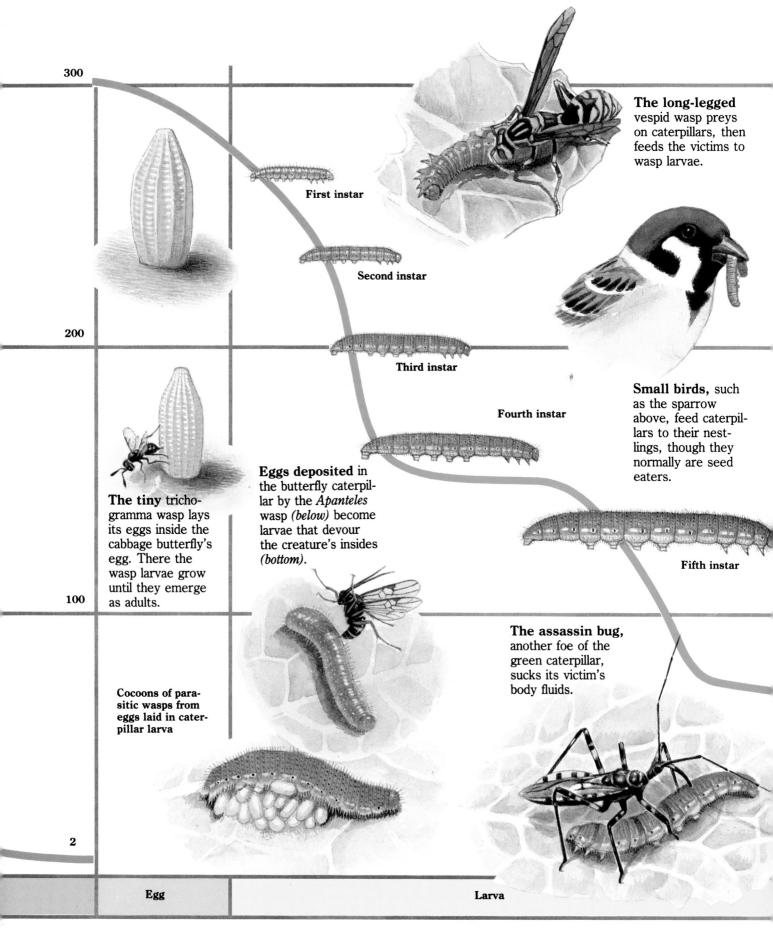

300

The long-legged vespid wasp preys on caterpillars, then feeds the victims to wasp larvae.

First instar

Second instar

200

Third instar

Fourth instar

Small birds, such as the sparrow above, feed caterpillars to their nestlings, though they normally are seed eaters.

The tiny trichogramma wasp lays its eggs inside the cabbage butterfly's egg. There the wasp larvae grow until they emerge as adults.

Eggs deposited in the butterfly caterpillar by the *Apanteles* wasp *(below)* become larvae that devour the creature's insides *(bottom)*.

Fifth instar

100

The assassin bug, another foe of the green caterpillar, sucks its victim's body fluids.

Cocoons of parasitic wasps from eggs laid in caterpillar larva

2

Egg

Larva

Insects' lives are so fraught with peril that it is surprising so many make it to maturity. On their way from egg to adult, they may be devoured by any number of predators, succumb to parasites or disease, or drown in heavy rains.

The graph below gives a brief overview of the natural enemies of the cabbage butterfly during each phase of its life cycle. An adult lays about 300 eggs. Those that hatch grow into green caterpillars, which molt five times before becoming pupae. On average, only two of the 300 eggs survive long enough to mature and reproduce.

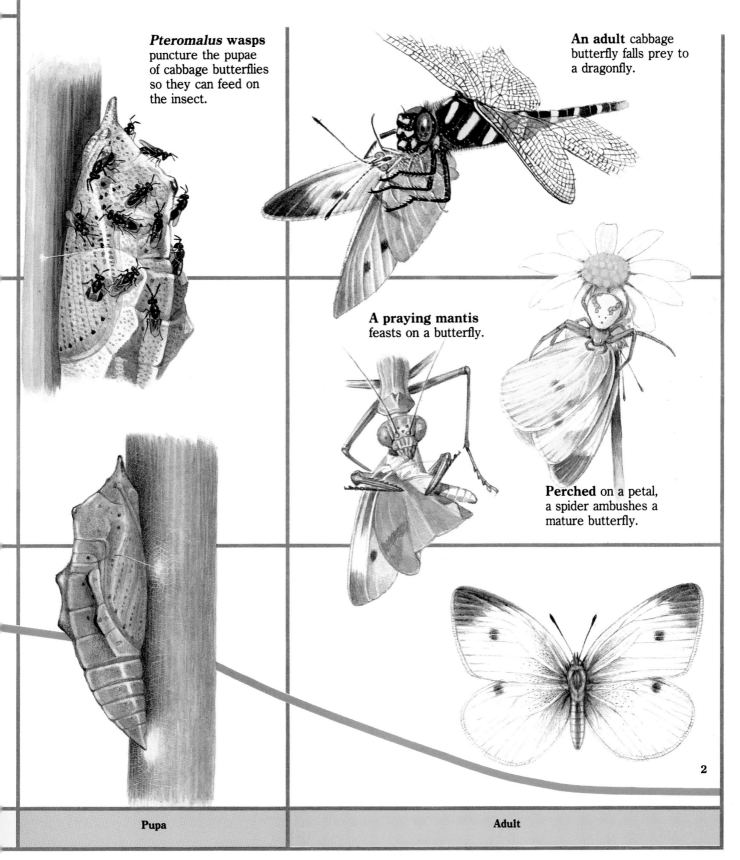

Pteromalus **wasps** puncture the pupae of cabbage butterflies so they can feed on the insect.

An adult cabbage butterfly falls prey to a dragonfly.

A praying mantis feasts on a butterfly.

Perched on a petal, a spider ambushes a mature butterfly.

2

| Pupa | Adult |

How Does Camouflage Work?

By enabling insects to mimic or blend in with the background, the special coloration known as camouflage helps conceal and protect them from predators. Some insects resemble their primary habitat not only in coloration but in form. The wings of certain butterflies and grasshoppers, for example, simulate the shape and veins of the leaves on which they usually rest. Other insects can be mistaken for blades of grass, flowers, bark, twigs, seed pods, or lichens.

Depending on their environment, some insects of the same species may sport markedly different camouflage garb. As long ago as 1850, scientists in England first noted the appearance

and spread of a dark mutant form of the light-colored peppered moth in areas where factories were spewing out black soot. Since then, the dark variants have come to predominate in polluted industrial areas, such as Birmingham. Elsewhere, however, they compose only a minority of the peppered moth population. In country districts, such as Dorset, the original mottled brown-and-gray form still prevails.

This phenomenon, known as industrial melanism, is a prime example of natural selection. The peppered moth is at a selective advantage, as experiments involving the release and recapture of both forms of this species have proved.

Normal peppered moths escape notice in country regions *(far left)* but are easy prey in industrial areas *(near left)*.

A matter of posture

Many moths display conspicuous vertical or horizontal markings on their wings. Tree bark has similar orientations. In order to be effectively concealed, the moth must align its wing patterns with the design of the bark.

Correct posture   **Wrong posture**

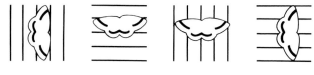

Correct posture   **Wrong posture**

A gray moth blends into the light background, while its dark relative stands out.

Can Insects Mimic Snakes?

Although few insects are more than 4 inches long, some of them are able to frighten off larger predators such as birds, lizards, or monkeys by mimicking the body shape and threatening posture of a snake. The eyelike markings of some caterpillars, for example, closely resemble the eyes of a snake. Scientists suggest that these tiny impersonators fool their enemies merely by making them think of real snakes.

At rest on a leaf *(above),* a silk moth caterpillar appears defenseless. An alarming surprise, however, awaits the hungry bird about to pounce on it *(right).*

Eying the enemy

Concentric rings that look like eyes mark the wings of many moths and some beetles. When threatened, these insects flash their eyespots to scare off enemies.

When its wings are spread and both eyespots revealed, the owl butterfly of South America resembles the face of an owl. In its everyday behavior, however, the insect rests with closed wings. Some entomologists believe the eyespots on the closed wings may protect the butterfly because they resemble the eyes of the tree frogs that prey on it.

At rest, the owl butterfly displays one eyespot on either side of its body.

The large tree frog may ignore the insect by mistaking it for another frog.

118

The caterpillar lifts its head to reveal a startling serpentlike eye design. Reminded of a snake about to strike, the attacking bird recoils.

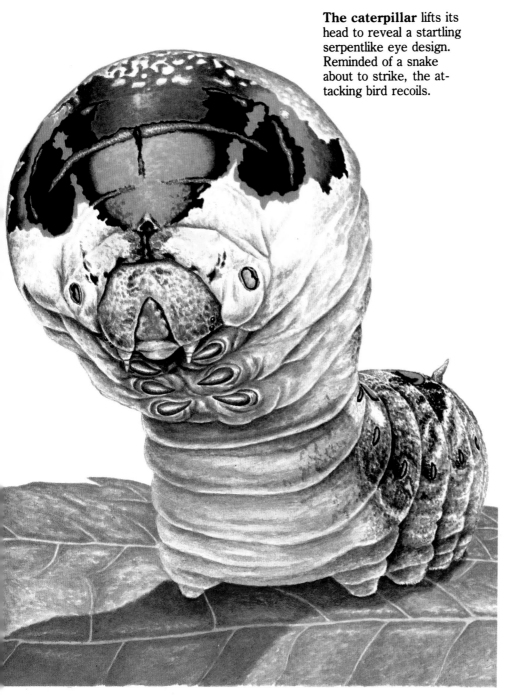

The eyespots and scalelike markings on the sparrow moth caterpillar lend it the menacing guise of a snake.

The silkworm moth from Japan may owe its survival to its wing tips, which some researchers think look like snake heads.

Faced by a predator, a caterpillar of the papilionid family of butterflies arches its upper body to reveal the alarming eyespots under its thorax.

Pint-size impostors

Less than 2 inches long, the planthopper of the Fulgoridae family *(right)* has an eyelike bump on its head that lends it the appearance of a miniature alligator. Reinforcing the disguise are distinctive markings along the lower part of the insect's head, which look like teeth. Despite its small size, the insect seems to have the same effect on potential predators that a real alligator would. When a planthopper was placed in a cage with a monkey, the monkey screamed and raced about in fright.

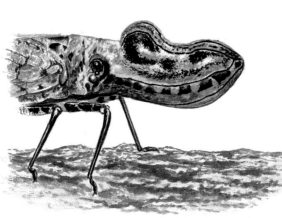

The planthopper's true eyes lie below and behind the bump on its head.

Its likeness to the alligator's fierce head may safeguard the small planthopper from insect eaters—such as birds and monkeys—that fear the bigger reptiles.

What Is Warning Coloration?

The bright and conspicuous colors that adorn the bodies of foul-tasting insects are called warning coloration. Most often sporting striking shades of yellow, red, or orange, such species have no need to hide, for they protect themselves with bad-smelling or poisonous secretions.

After a few encounters with these undesirable insects, most predators learn to avoid them—a task that is made simple by their distinctive warning coloration. In a phenomenon known as mimicry, a number of harmless insects enjoy similar protection merely by looking like the inedible species. Potential predators tend to shun any creatures that bear markings similar to the distasteful creatures.

An unsuspecting skink sinks its teeth into a *Pryeria sinica* caterpillar, which immediately secretes a bitter-tasting fluid.

An array of warning colors

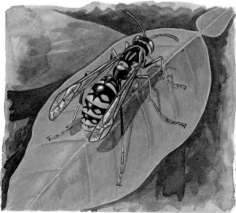

The wasp's yellow and black stripes typical of stinging bees are quickly recognized by other creatures—including human beings—who fear their venom.

The tortoise ladybug and its relatives secrete a bitter fluid. Although their patterns and colors vary, all types of ladybugs stand out in vivid hues.

A red, yellow, and black color scheme distinguishes the akagi stink bug. The insect keeps away predators by emitting a formidable stench.

Recoiling from the caterpillar's repulsive taste, the lizard releases its victim.

After several such unpleasant experiences, the lizard recognizes the caterpillar's warning coloration and shuns the insect.

Yellow stripes and red spots distinguish poisonous *Idea leuconoe* caterpillars. The caterpillars feed on plants that are toxic to vertebrates.

Red and yellow patches of South America's *Heliconius* butterfly announce that it consumes poisonous plants and passes the toxins along to predators.

Marked by an hourglass design on its back, the Oriental saddleback caterpillar punishes predators with painful stings from the poisonous hairs ringing its body.

Which Insect Sprays Poisonous Gas?

To drive away enemies, bombardier beetles squirt a mist of scalding chemicals. So noxious is the substance that most predators, including birds, toads, reptiles, and rodents, abandon their attack when subjected to it. The ingredients of the blistering solution, hydroquinone and hydrogen peroxide, are secreted separately by special glands in the beetle's abdomen. The chemicals are stored in an abdominal chamber until the insect is attacked, at which point they flow into a second, thick-walled chamber. There an enzyme catalyzes a reaction between the two chemicals that produces the corrosive substance quinone— a chemical used in tanning leather—along with the oxygen necessary to blast the poison out the tip of the abdomen.

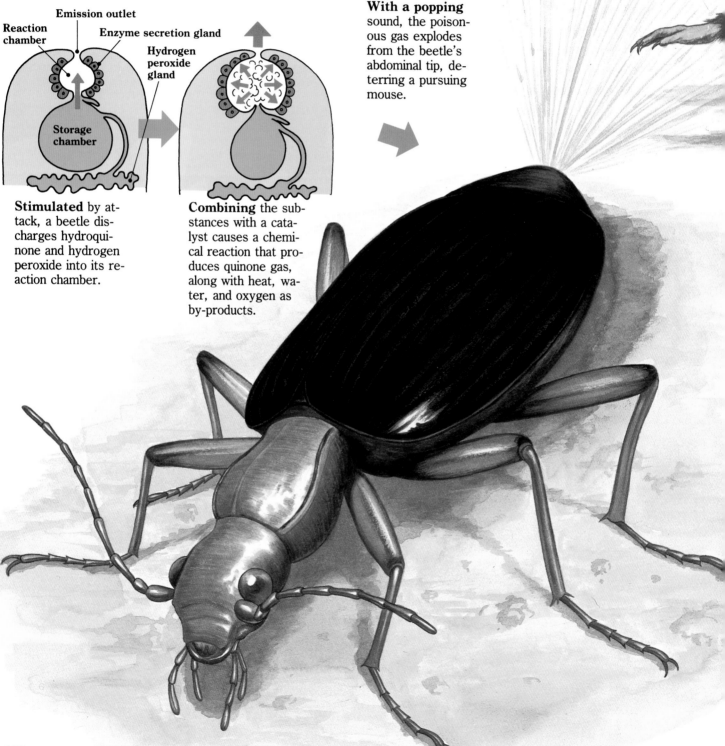

Reaction chamber

Emission outlet

Enzyme secretion gland

Hydrogen peroxide gland

Storage chamber

Stimulated by attack, a beetle discharges hydroquinone and hydrogen peroxide into its reaction chamber.

Combining the substances with a catalyst causes a chemical reaction that produces quinone gas, along with heat, water, and oxygen as by-products.

With a popping sound, the poisonous gas explodes from the beetle's abdominal tip, deterring a pursuing mouse.

Swiveling its abdominal tip forward, a bombardier beetle shoots a cloud of poisonous gas at a threatening human finger. The insect can aim its irritating spray in any direction.

Chemical warfare

Bombardier beetles are not the only insects to defend themselves with chemical weapons. Some species of sugar bugs, for example, secrete a poisonous liquid, which they rub onto would-be predators. And the vinegarroon scorpion emits a vinegary odor when pursued.

Many groups of stink bugs spray a rank-smelling liquid containing formaldehyde to ward off enemies. The caterpillar of the swallowtail butter-fly also employs offensive odor in its defense.

Some worker and soldier termites secrete a poisonous adhesive to defend their nest. Faced with invaders, these insects intentionally burst their abdomens in order to spray the sticky toxin at the enemy.

An abdominal odor gland produces the stink bug's gas.

Some worker ants spray blistering streams of formic acid at their enemies.

The vinegarroon scorpion pivots its segmented tail to direct a spray of acetic acid.

The swallowtail butterfly caterpillar exudes a fetid substance from a horn-like scent gland called the osmeterium.

Why Do Bees and Wasps Sting?

Social bees and wasps, which live and raise their young in colonies, use their venomous stingers to defend their hive or nest against invaders. At the first sign of attack, for example, eager armies of black hornets *(below)* swarm from the nest to sting the enemy with their poison. Predators of all sizes, from birds to bears, generally retreat from the painful onslaught.

Some solitary wasps rely on their stingers not only for defense but to provide food for their larvae. The insects' venom paralyzes their prey— usually spiders or caterpillars.

Evolution of the stinger

The stinger arming bees and wasps evolved from the egg-laying tube, or ovipositor, that their ancestors used to deposit eggs inside plants or other insects. In insects of the order Hymenoptera such as the horntail and the ichneumon flies, the ovipositor retains its original function. For many species, however, the tube eventually came to secrete poison, which the insects used to paralyze prey to feed their larvae. Over time bees and wasps who feed solely on pollen and nectar developed a stinger that is purely a defensive organ.

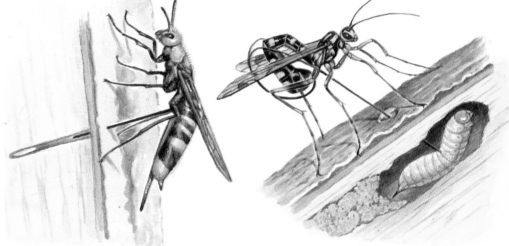

A horntail inserts its ovipositor into a tree trunk to lay eggs. Its larvae will feed on the wood.

An ichneumon fly drills through timber with its ovipositor to deposit eggs in the larva of another insect.

Struggling to pull its stinger out of an enemy, a honeybee ruptures its abdomen and soon dies. Left behind, the stinger continues to inject venom.

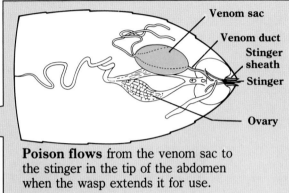

Venom sac
Venom duct
Stinger sheath
Stinger
Ovary

Poison flows from the venom sac to the stinger in the tip of the abdomen when the wasp extends it for use.

How a bee stings

The bee's stinger consists of a hard, narrow tube called the stylet and two barbed projections called lancets. When the insect stings, the lancets quickly slice into the victim and the venom is injected from the stylet into the wound. Because its barbs snag in the victim's flesh, the stinger is ripped from the bee when the insect pulls away.

Stylet

Lancet

To provision the larvae in its burrow, the digger wasp paralyzes a caterpillar with its stinger.

The nest-dwelling long-legged wasp deters predators—here a monkey—with its formidable sting.

When stinging an enemy, the honeybee secretes a pheromone to summon reinforcements.

How Do Ants Fight?

Armed with a pair of powerful mandibles and an arsenal of poisonous chemicals *(below)*, ants are well equipped for combat. Not only do they fight and kill the small insects on which they prey, ants must also defend their colonies against those who prey on them, including birds, lizards, termites, and some mammals.

The tiny warriors' most common opponents, however, are other ants. As a colony expands, its workers must venture increasingly farther from the nest to collect enough food for the growing population. Sooner or later, they are bound to trespass on another colony's territory. The resulting territorial battles can pit armies of different species or the same species against each other. Conflicts between different species often end with a fight to the death. Sometimes the victors even carry their dead enemies back to the nest for food.

Black carpenter ants from warring nests confront each other by displaying their mandibles and raising their thoraxes. During territorial battles, so many ants are killed that their bodies lie in heaps after the fight.

The ant's arsenal

An ant's mandibles, or jaws, are among its most effective weapons. Varying in shape and size from one species to the next, mandibles can hold or pinch an enemy in a viselike grip. Some mandibles are sharp enough to slice through an enemy's skin or shell; others can crush or even clip off a limb.

Poisons also play a major role in ant combat. Some families of ants are equipped with stingers in the tips of their abdomens. These powerful attack weapons inject venoms potent enough to kill other insects. So fierce is the sting of some species, such as those of the *Paraponera* genus of South America, that it can be crippling even to humans.

Other ants have no stingers but eject their poison as a spray. The venom's main ingredient, formic acid, causes burning and itching in humans and is particularly effective against small animals.

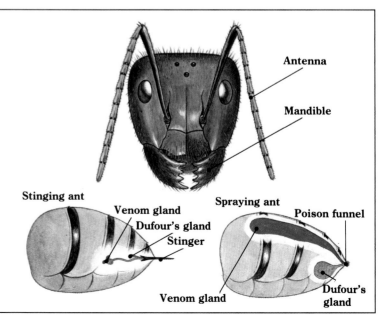

Antenna

Mandible

Stinging ant

Venom gland
Dufour's gland
Stinger

Venom gland

Spraying ant

Poison funnel

Dufour's gland

Twice the size of its attackers, a black mountain ant struggles in vain against several red ants as they bite it to death. The smaller ants' superior numbers prevent their larger victim from retaliating effectively.

Yellowtail ants spray a sticky poisonous liquid, secreted by the Dufour's gland, at their enemies. The ant's swiveling abdomen allows it to aim the venom.

Defending the nest

Nesting in mounds of fallen larch needles, the *Formica yessensis* ant is particularly adept at repelling its foes with formic acid. As soon as an enemy approaches the anthill, the insect assumes battle posture, thrusting its abdomen upward between its hind legs. When the invader is 7 inches away or closer, the ant squirts it with a stream of formic acid from the tip of its abdomen. Small insects are easily killed by the acid defense.

Not all predators, however, are so easily deterred. A bear, for example, can break up an anthill and lick up tens of thousands of its inhabitants before the insects even begin to respond to the attack.

6
The Complex Lives of Social Insects

Many kinds of insects care for their young. But species called social insects lavish prolonged care on their young and spend most of their lives in large family groups called colonies. Many familiar insects live in such social groups; among them are ants, bees, wasps, and termites. Each social insect species has evolved a particular way of life, with special ways of getting food and unique nest-building methods. Within this intricate social structure, a colony of insects—ants, for instance—may support up to 22 million individuals working together.

In every insect society, the colony members are closely related. Often just one female, called the queen, lays the eggs from which all other members of the colony hatch. Queen ants, bees, and wasps mate as young adults and then lay eggs for a lifetime; queen termites mate repeatedly with the king.

The queen's offspring play different roles in the society. Workers build the nest and gather food. They also feed and tend the young and usually the queen as well. Soldier ants, soldier termites, and soldier aphids protect the colony. To keep a colony running smoothly, social insects must communicate. Ants lay down scent trails, and honeybee scouts use a complex dance language to tell nest mates where to find food or sites for new nests.

Members of insect colonies share the labor. Honeybee scouts *(above)* dance in figure eights and circles to tell other workers about a new food source. A winged termite king and queen *(below)* start a new colony, after digging a hole and mating.

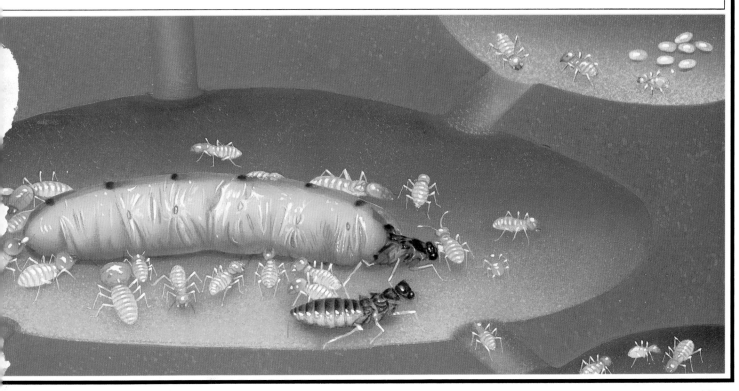

Which Insects Live in Families?

Some insects merely drop their eggs and fly away. Others, the social insects, build elaborate homes where hordes of relatives nurse eggs and young and defend them from enemies. Between these extremes lies a wide range of insect family behavior.

Many species lay eggs where hatchlings have the best chance to survive, on food plants or in buried balls of food. A few insects live for a time in small family units—usually only a female and her offspring—in which the female keeps her eggs clean and safe. But in several kinds of beetles, the males also share in the rearing of offspring, as in the bess beetles, dung beetles, and bark beetles, shown below and at right.

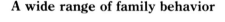

Home in the log. Bess beetles tunnel into fallen trees, where they live in colonies. The male and female, shiny, black, and about 1¼ inches long, mix rotten wood with saliva to feed their grubs.

Buried with food. Dung beetles bury balls of mammal dung. The female lays an egg inside, giving the larva a safe place to grow and plenty of food. Until the larva becomes an adult, both parents stay with it.

A wide range of family behavior

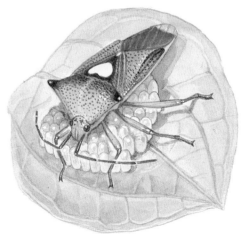

The migratory grasshopper lays clumps of eggs in small holes in the soil. After laying the eggs, the female abandons them.

The swallowtail butterfly also lays her eggs and then leaves. But she lays eggs only on plants the young can use for food.

The half-inch-long female stink bug lays large groups of barrel-shaped eggs, then stays with them to defend them against predators.

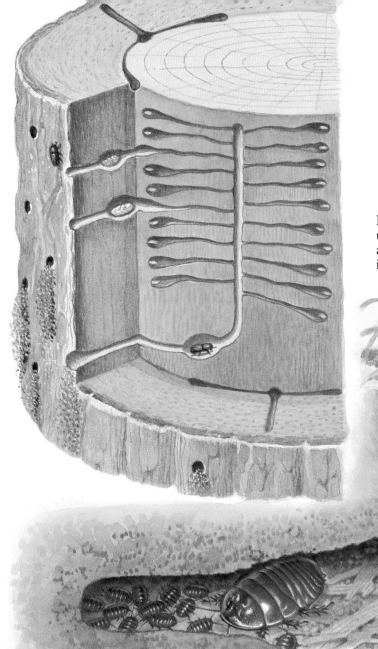

Adult bark beetle

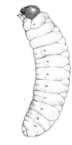

Larva of bark beetle

Bark tunnelers. Bark beetles bore into the soft tissue under the bark of living or dead trees. There they mate and lay eggs. The female feeds the young on fungus grown in the tunnels, while the male guards the main entrance.

Leafy den. Three-inch-long Australian cockroaches pull leaves into their burrow to feed their young. Adults repel predators such as centipedes.

Feeding and protecting young

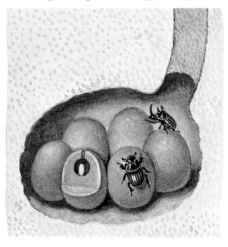

Dung beetles prepare a nursery for their young. The female lays eggs in a ball of dung and oversees the feeding of the growing grubs.

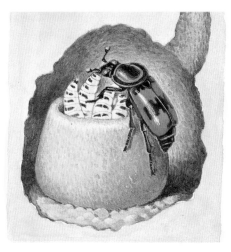

Burying beetles shape decaying flesh into balls to roll into their burrows. The young will hatch there, tended by the female.

Lifetime care

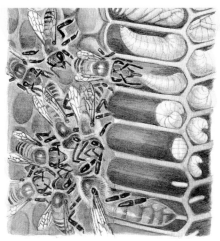

Honeybees, the true social insects, live in big families. The queen *(bottom)* lays the eggs, and worker bees care for her and the young.

How Is a Queen Honeybee Born?

The queen is surrounded by workers who feed and groom her. In the process, they lick off queen substance, a secretion that regulates their behavior.

A honeybee queen hatches from the same kind of egg as a worker, but she grows in a large egg chamber *(below, bottom)* and is fed a special diet. New queens are normally produced in late spring, when a hive becomes crowded with up to 80,000 workers. Then a chemical produced by the queen—queen substance—that prevents workers from producing new queens, has to be shared by more workers, who each receive less than normal. In response, workers build queen cells, in which the old queen lays eggs. When she has filled the queen cells, she flies off with a swarm of workers to start a new colony.

By late spring, the hive gets crowded, and there is less queen substance to go around. The queen is fed less food, loses weight, and lays fewer eggs.

A signal to divide the hive. When workers get less queen substance than usual, they build special egg chambers—the queen cells—at the bottom of the combs.

A crop of queens. Once workers have made several queen cells, the queen lays one egg in each cell. This way, several new queens may mature at about the same time.

Special food. After these eggs hatch, nurse worker bees feed the larvae royal jelly. This protein-rich secretion helps the new queens grow faster than other larvae do.

A swarm leaves the hive

When a queen leaves the hive, a great many workers follow her in a swarm. The newly hatched queens may form their own swarms. Sometimes only a third of the workers remain in the old hive with one of the new queens. Each swarm alights on a tree and waits for scouts to find a suitable place in which to build a new nest.

As an old queen is laying eggs in the queen cells, workers begin to feed her less so that she will be able to fly.

If two unmated queens occupy the nest at the same time, one will kill the other. Queens rarely sting unless fighting other queens.

Capping the queen cell. Just before a queen larva matures, workers cap the cell with wax. They store enough food in the cell to feed the larva until it changes to a pupa.

A new queen. Only 16 days after being laid, the egg has turned from larva to pupa to queen. Soon she will fly out of the hive to mate with several drones.

Fertilized queen. A new queen will destroy any queen cells that are still occupied and, if other queens have emerged, may fight to the death for rule of the colony.

Do Bees Have a Language?

Though honeybees make a variety of sounds, they do not communicate with words. But a worker that finds a patch of nectar-rich flowers can tell other workers how to get there. Instead of talking, it dances to tell its audience how far away the flowers are and in which direction they must fly. Workers dance only in nests full of other workers; the others crowd around, sometimes joining the dance. Because the hive is dark inside, the "watching" workers actually get information by feeling the dancer with their antennae and from vibrations through the honeycomb.

Honeybees use three basic dances. One is a wide figure eight called the waggle dance, in which the dancer shakes its abdomen from side to side. The other dances are a round dance and a busy, buzzing dance. Only the waggle dance tells workers how to find a certain spot. The round dance excites them to hunt for food near the nest. And the workers do the buzzing dance to regulate two different colony activities, foraging and swarming. Scout bees in a swarm also use the waggle dance to tell about new nesting sites they have seen.

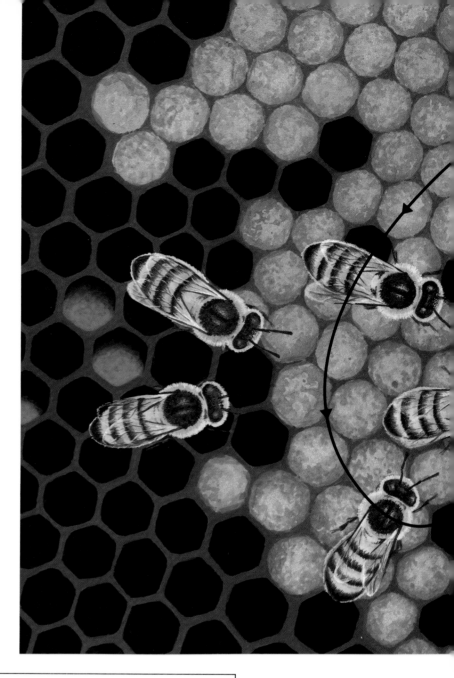

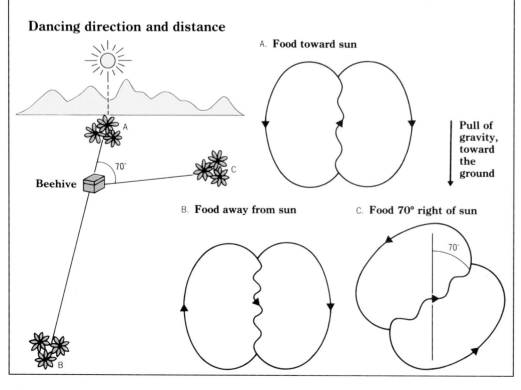

Dancing direction and distance

A. **Food toward sun**

B. **Food away from sun**

C. **Food 70° right of sun**

Pull of gravity, toward the ground

Beehive

Foraging bees indicate direction, distance, and quality of a food source by dancing. Dancers normally perform on vertical surfaces in the dark hive, using gravity to stand for the sun when they tell direction.

If a food source lies toward the sun (A), the dancer waggles straight up. If the food is off to the right of the sun (C), the bee angles its waggle. It can also convey the distance from the hive to the food (B), measured by how hard it worked to get there. To indicate hard work and long distance, the bee adds more waggles and slows the whole dance down. A lackluster dance indicates a poor food source, whereas an excited one tells of a treasure trove.

Workers may watch five or more dances before trying to find the food. Even then, fewer than half succeed.

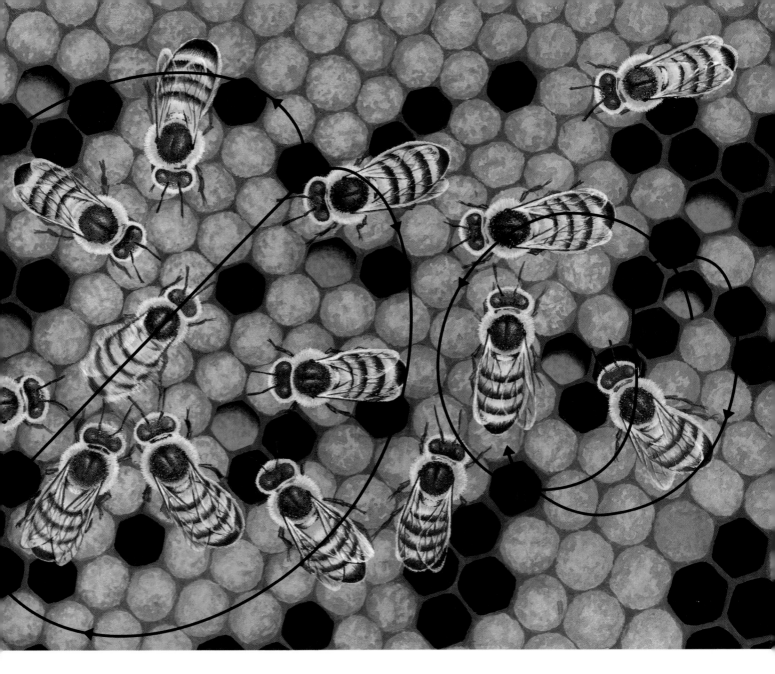

Finding a new nest site

In late spring honeybee nests become crowded with workers, and the cells of the comb fill up with honey and eggs. The old queen leaves the hive with a swarm of workers. They alight on a tree *(left)* and surround the queen with a temporary shelter that is made entirely of worker bees. Then workers begin scouting out sites to build a new nest.

A worker that has discovered food more than 100 yards away gives specific directions with a waggle dance *(above, left)*. It circles halfway around, crosses the circle with a waggle, then completes the circle. Other workers may dance with it.

When a scout finds a food source less than 100 yards from the hive, it dances in a circle *(above, right)*. This round dance excites other workers to search nearby. But the dance gives no more information about direction or distance.

What Are Africanized Honeybees?

According to some headlines, a foreign horde of so-called killer bees is invading North America. But these headlines tell only part of the truth. Africanized honeybees—sometimes referred to as killer bees—have spread north from South America to the southern United States. Since 1956 Africanized honeybees have caused as many as a thousand deaths in South and Central America. But these bees are no more foreign and as individuals not much more danger-ous than common North American honeybees.

Early settlers of North America brought mild-mannered European honeybees with them, and some time later, beekeepers imported other strains to improve their stocks. In 1956 a Brazil-ian scientist, hoping to breed a strain that would thrive in the tropics, imported an African race of honeybees. The African honeybees did thrive; they made lots of honey and swarmed often. Some escaped and bred with local bees as they

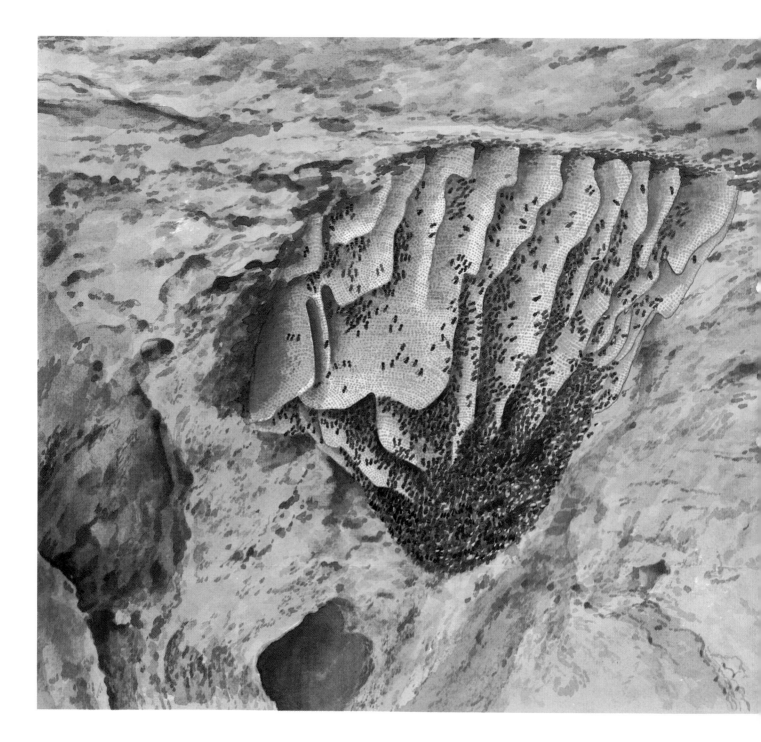

spread north and south. Then their defensive behavior came to light, and their name eventually changed to killer bees. When their hive is disturbed, Africanized bees will launch a fierce stinging defense of their home and may give the intruder thousands of stings. But in fact their venom is no more poisonous than that of North American honeybees, and the smaller Africanized honeybees actually inject a third less venom when they sting. Like all honeybees, Africanized honeybees can sting only once—then they die. Even with Africanized honeybees on the scene, people are less likely to be killed by any insect than by lightning.

Nearly identical. Though Africanized honeybees *(left)* are slightly smaller than North American honeybees *(right)*, it takes an expert eye and good measuring tools to tell them apart.

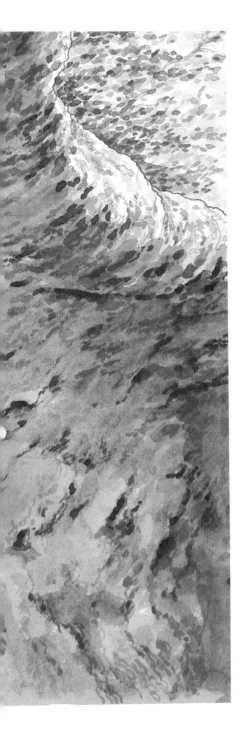

How the bees spread

From southern Brazil, where the first African bees escaped in 1956, Africanized bees have spread, traveling about 250 miles a year. They were in Central America by 1981 and the United States by 1990. In 1992 scientists trapped Africanized honeybees in San Antonio, Texas. The bees stopped their southward spread in temperate Argentina in 1976, leading some scientists to predict they will not reach the northern part of North America.

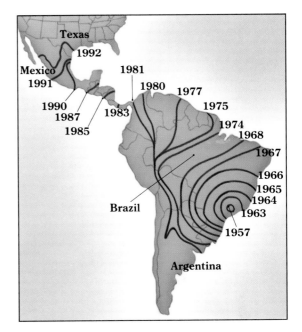

Identifying honeybees

To determine which species of bee has been caught, an entomologist *(right)* feeds enlarged wing images into a computer. Africanized bees' wings are slightly smaller than those of North American bees.

Ready to sting. A wild Africanized honeybee nest *(left)* hangs from a cave roof. In such close quarters, an animal—or a person—may be unable to escape the thousands of bees that are defending their nest.

How Do Ants Live in Colonies?

All ants live in social groups, but ant colonies vary greatly. In adapting to almost every environment on Earth, ants—estimated at up to 20,000 species—have developed many different ways of life. Some species form colonies containing only a queen, a dozen or so workers, and a few males. In such colonies, all the ants look much alike and may share jobs. At the other extreme, a colony of African driver ants may have up to 100 queens laying eggs continuously and as many as 22 million workers. They cooperate so well that the colony seems almost like a "superorganism"—a single huge living thing. Many complex colonies contain several specialized kinds of workers, each doing a different job.

Storage. Desert-dwelling honeypot ants gather food and return home with crops so full that they are distended like balloons. They hang from the roof of their nest and let ordinary workers feed from them.

Slavemakers. Several ant species, such as those of the *Polyergus* genus, capture the young of other ants to raise and keep as servants. Some species of so-called slavemakers cannot survive without their captives to feed them and care for their young.

Leaf cutters
grow fungus.

Stitchers. Most ants nest underground, but some build high in the trees. First, living bridges of ants pull leaves together. Then workers "sew" the leaves—using larvae to lay down threads of the same silk they spin for cocoons.

Farmers. Leaf-cutting ants grow their food in huge underground nests. Workers cut bits of leaves and carry them to the nest, where they compost leaves and droppings. A special fungus grows on the compost. All life stages eat only this fungus.

Warriors. Australian bulldog ants are well named. More than an inch long with huge jaws, these ants bite and hold on while they jab with a ¼-inch-long stinger. They can jump nearly a foot while protecting the nest or chasing prey. Their colonies contain no more than 2,000 ants, and the queens receive no special attention.

What Are Termite Societies Like?

Termites live in social colonies of up to two million members. Their colonies may look much like those of ants, but termites are more closely related to cockroaches. Termites differ from other social insects—the bees and wasps—in several ways. They emerge from eggs as nymphs rather than larvae. A termite queen mates repeatedly to keep producing eggs and in some species can lay 86,000 eggs a day. Large and small workers of both sexes supply the colony with food and build mounds or underground nests. Large and small soldiers use jaws—or in some species, special glue-squirting heads—to defend the nest from ants. Most termites never see the light, for the nest is sealed except when young winged kings and queens fly out to mate and start new nests.

Eggs

Winged male

Winged female

Ants raid a termite colony

Termites eat mostly cellulose: vegetation, wood, and soil. Aboveground, the workers *(far right)* are exposed to attack by many predators. Small soldier termites *(middle)* may go along to protect the workers. Here Ponerine ants, which march in companies of about 100 workers, attack termites on the surface. Ponerine ants will also invade mounds to capture termites. Each ant will carry three or four termites back to the ant colony to use as food.

In the royal chamber

Termite colonies consist of a network of tunnels and chambers. One of the largest is the royal chamber, where, in some termite species, the king and queen spend most of their lives. Workers feed and clean the royal pair and carry away eggs. The queen's swollen body weighs more than a pencil. She can lay tens of thousands of eggs a day.

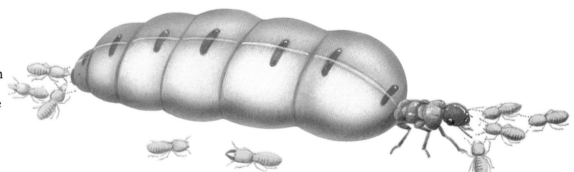

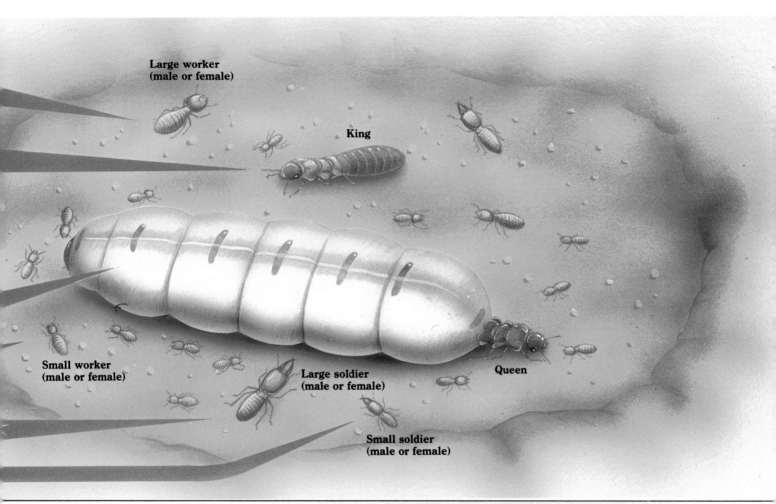

Large worker
(male or female)

King

Small worker
(male or female)

Large soldier
(male or female)

Queen

Small soldier
(male or female)

Natural enemies. The driver ants of Africa pose the biggest threat to African termite colonies. Huge columns of these inch-long workers and soldiers travel for long distances, capturing every insect in their way. Driver ants can also invade termite colonies. The driver ants search every tunnel and chamber, devouring the king and queen termites as well as many thousands of workers. A driver-ant raid can wipe out an entire termite colony.

How Do Termites Build Their Nests?

Termites are among the most successful of insect species in tropical grasslands. Some, like the fungus-growing termites on these pages, build mounds 20 feet high, with elaborate networks of tunnels in and around them. The termite colony cycle begins when thousands of young winged males and females fly out of a mound in the fall. Settling to the ground within 100 yards of their home mound, most are eaten by birds, mammals, and even humans. The few that survive shed their wings and start a new colony *(below)*. Four years of egg laying will pass before winged males and females leave this nest to found a new colony.

A mound of fungus-growing termites

Founders. The male and female have shed their wings. The male follows the female to a site where they dig a hole and mate.

How the new colony grows

After a winter underground, the new queen *(near right)* lays her first eggs, which hatch into tiny workers *(far right)*. As soon as the workers can feed themselves, they begin to care for the king, queen, new eggs, and newly hatched young. The swollen queen may lay 30,000 eggs a day for 10 or more years.

Colony growth. Eggs laid later hatch into specialized soldier and worker termites. The workers feed the royal pair and enlarge the mound.

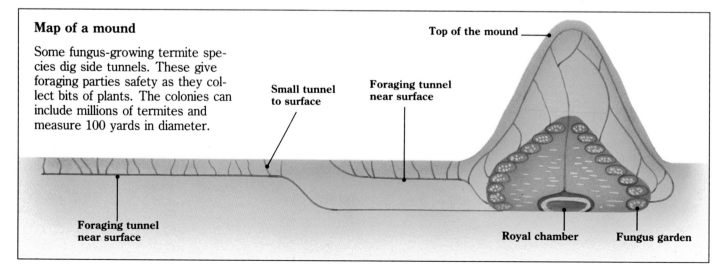

Map of a mound

Some fungus-growing termite species dig side tunnels. These give foraging parties safety as they collect bits of plants. The colonies can include millions of termites and measure 100 yards in diameter.

Top of the mound

Small tunnel to surface

Foraging tunnel near surface

Foraging tunnel near surface

Royal chamber

Fungus garden

Air conditioning and a garden

At the center of a fungus-growing termite mound are large fungus gardens. Workers build these ball-shaped structures from their own droppings, adding chewed plant material and saliva. On this compost grows a special fungus, which the termites eat. The fungus helps the termites digest the wood they feed on. The compost also creates heat, helping to ventilate the mound (*right*).

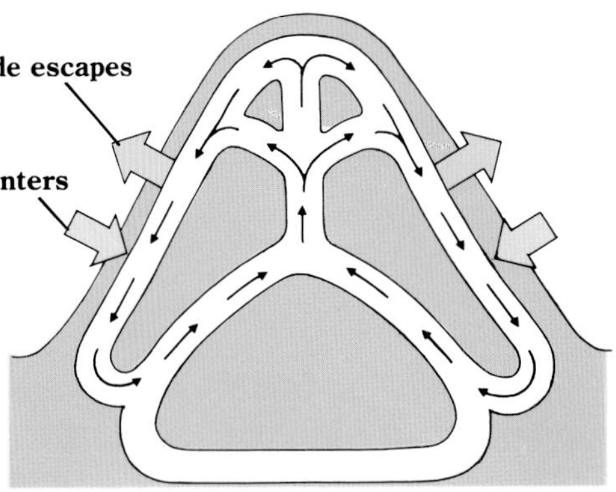

Carbon dioxide escapes

Oxygen enters

Ventilation. Rising heat circulates air in the tunnels. The thin dirt walls let oxygen in and carbon dioxide out.

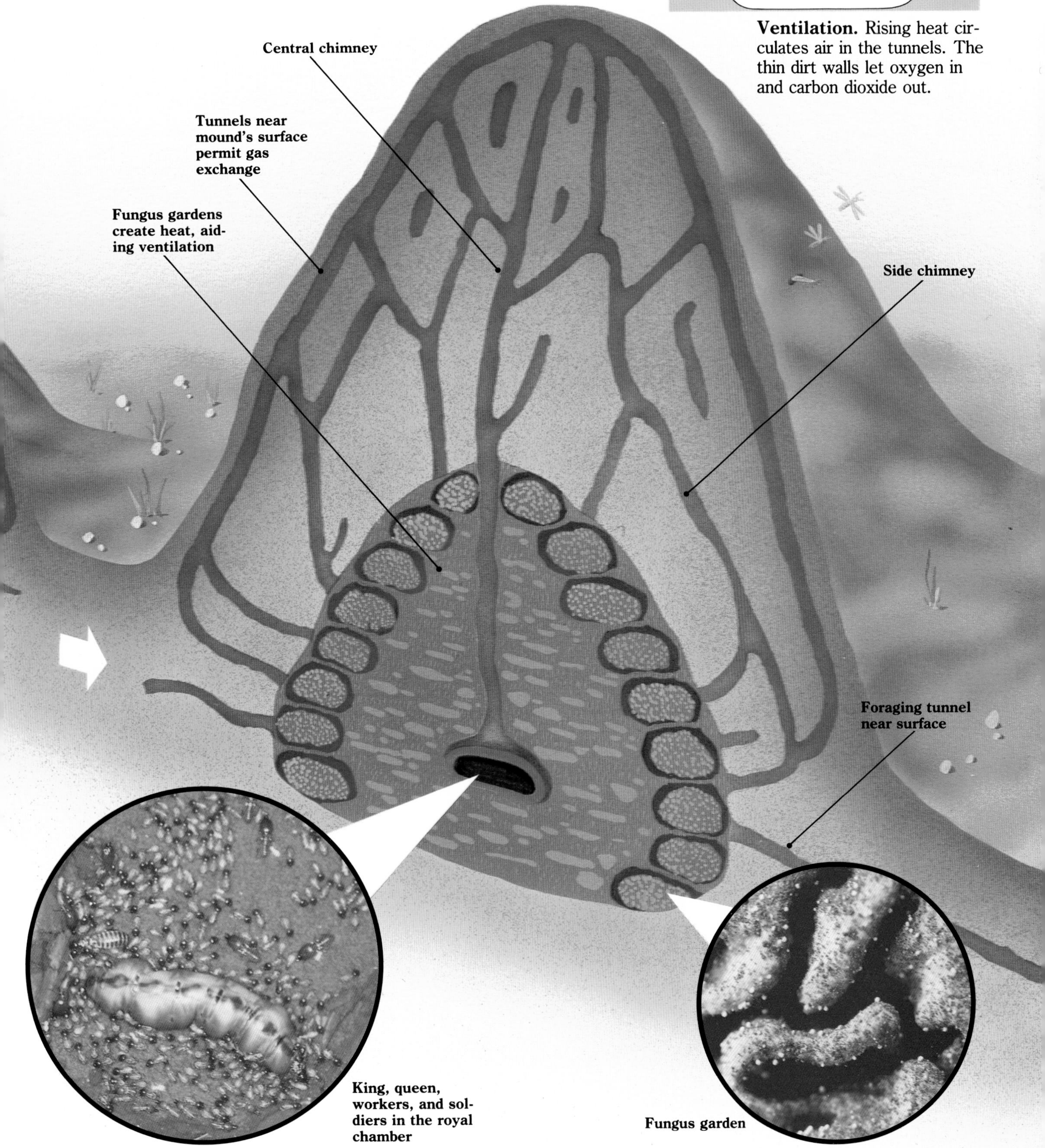

Central chimney

Tunnels near mound's surface permit gas exchange

Fungus gardens create heat, aiding ventilation

Side chimney

Foraging tunnel near surface

King, queen, workers, and soldiers in the royal chamber

Fungus garden

Can Aphids Defend Themselves?

Soft-bodied and often wingless, aphids are easy prey for many insects. The larvae of the ladybug and Asian flower fly, in fact, eat little else, and the caterpillar of the *Dipha aphidivora* moth drags aphids into its cocoon. But one aphid species—Alexander's horned aphid—fights back with soldiers. They grow hard, armorlike exoskeletons, long, strong front legs, and stiletto-like mouthparts. To defend the colony, these larger soldiers swarm onto a predator, such as the flower fly larva below. There they cling with their forelegs and stab with their mouthparts until the overwhelmed attacker falls to the ground, taking the defending soldiers with it. In another strategy, they crush the flower fly eggs. Although the gains of the tiny soldiers against giant predators seem small, they slow down the enemies enough so the species can survive.

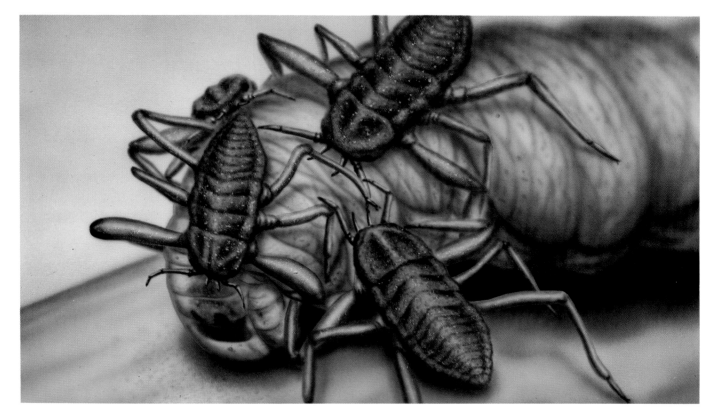

Soldier aphids and foes

Soldier aphids fail against some predators. Giant ladybugs' exoskeletons withstand attack, and dwarf ladybugs' snowy wax coat makes soldiers ignore them. But the spiny larvae of giant ladybugs and newly hatched larvae of flower flies can become victims of soldier aphids.

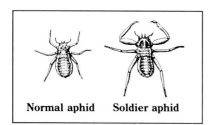

Normal aphid   Soldier aphid

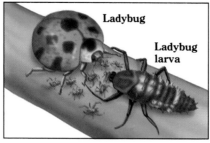

Adult ladybug and larva attack aphids.

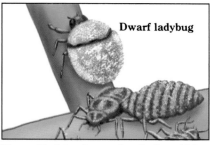

Dwarf ladybug's coating fools aphids.

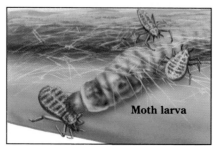

Moth larva strikes from its cocoon.

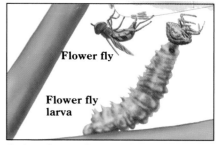

Asian flower fly larva feeds on aphid.

Glossary

Abdomen: The rear section of an insect body, located behind the thorax, that contains the digestive and reproductive organs.

Aciniformes gland: The gland in spiders that produces silk used to wrap up prey.

Alary muscles: A set of muscles, located around an insect's dorsal vessel, that help control the flow of blood by contracting and relaxing.

Annelida: The phylum consisting of the segmented worms.

Antenna: A sensory organ, located on the heads of insects, used to detect smells, air movement, and vibrations.

Aorta: In insects, the main blood vessel leading from the heart toward the head.

Arthropod: A member of a phylum of invertebrate animals that have segmented bodies, jointed limbs, and a skeleton on the outside of the body; includes insects, spiders, and crustaceans.

Articular membrane: The flexible area between two regions of hardened exoskeleton that forms the joints in arthropods.

Axon: A nerve fiber; the part of the nerve cell that transmits impulses.

Beetle: An insect that has two pairs of wings, with the front pair usually modified into a stiff outer pair of wing cases.

Biological classification: A system scientists developed to group organisms together by their natural relationships. The categories, going from the most inclusive to the most specific, are: kingdom, phylum, class, order, family, genus, and species.

Bug: A member of the insect order Hemiptera. All bugs are insects, but not all insects are bugs.

Chrysalis: The pupa of a moth or butterfly.

Cibarial pump: A mosquito mouthpart; the pump that draws up blood from its prey.

Cilia: Short, hairlike structures.

Class: A category of biological classification between phylum and order; includes related orders.

Colony: A group of social insects that share a nest.

Corneagen layer: A portion of the insect eye that is secreted by the corneagen cell.

Corneal lens: The lens that covers each ommatidium of a compound eye. A dragonfly may have as many as 10,000 in each eye.

Coxa: The part of the insect leg that attaches to the thorax.

Cribellum: A structure found in certain spiders that produces a fluffy-looking silk used to catch prey.

Crop: A pouch in the foregut of an insect where food is stored.

Cuticle: The hard noncellular material that makes up the exoskeleton in insects.

Dendrite: The portion of the nerve cell specialized for the reception of stimuli that are then transmitted by the axon.

Dorsal: Located along the back or upper side.

Dorsal sac: A modified gastric cecum.

Dorsal vessel: The tube that acts like a heart to pump blood, or hemolymph, through an insect's body.

Exocrine system: The glands that discharge secretions into ducts that carry them to the organs where they are needed.

Exoskeleton: A skeleton that is on the outside of an arthropod's body. Muscles are attached to the inside of the exoskeleton.

Extensor muscle: A muscle in an appendage of an insect that works with flexor muscles to straighten a part of the body.

Family: A category of biological classification between genus and order; includes related genuses.

Femur: The upper part of the insect leg and the most muscular, located between the tibia and the coxa; one of the four main parts of the insect leg along with the tarsus, tibia, and coxa.

Flagellum: The end section of the insect antenna.

Flexor muscle: A muscle in an appendage of an insect that works with extensor muscles to bend a part of the body.

Frenulum: A thin band of bristles linking the hind wing to the forewing in moths and a few butterflies.

Fulcrum: The function of that portion of the body structure that acts as a support or pivot for insect wings.

Ganglion: One of several nerve bundles, or nerve centers, that together with the brain and the nerve cord form an insect's central nervous system.

Gastric cecum: A pouch in the midgut that aids digestion.

Genus: A category of biological classification between family and species, composed of species that are structurally related.

Gill: In insects, the structure through which aquatic nymphs obtain oxygen and discharge carbon dioxide.

Gland: A specialized group of cells that produce and secrete a substance used by the organism.

Gregarious insects: Insects that congregate.

Hormone: A chemical produced in small amounts that enters the bloodstream and is carried to some other part or organ where it has a specific effect.

Hypermetamorphosis: Stages of development in addition to those in complete metamorphosis.

Hypopharynx: A tonguelike structure in the mouth of an insect, from which the salivary glands open.

Insect: A class of arthropods that have a head, thorax, and abdomen, three pairs of legs, and usually one or two pairs of wings.

Instar: The stage between molts in immature arthropods.

Invertebrate: An animal that lacks a backbone.

Johnston's organ: An organ of the insect antenna that perceives vibrations.

Kingdom: The largest category of biological classification. All living and fossil organisms are currently divided into five kingdoms: Monera (bacteria), Protista (one-celled eukaryotes), Fungi, Plantae, and Animalia.

Labellum: An extension on the lower end of the labium in certain species of flies.

Labium: The lower lip of an insect.

Labrum: The upper lip of an insect.

Larva: The immature stage of an insect that goes through complete metamorphosis. It is the stage between egg and pupa in which the form differs greatly from the adult. Caterpillar, grub, and maggot are names of larvae of different species.

Lateral: Located along the side.

Levator: A muscle that helps to raise a part of the body such as a leg; works with depressor muscles.

Malpighian tubule: A structure in an insect's abdomen, located near the junction of the midgut and hindgut, that is involved in excretion and helps to regulate the internal balance of salt and water.

Mandible: One of the front pair of insect mouthparts, which often act like jaws.

Maxilla: One of the paired mouthparts behind the mandibles.

Metamorphosis: The change in form of an organism during development. In **complete metamorphosis** an insect goes through distinct egg, larval, and pupal stages before becoming an adult. In **incomplete metamorphosis** an insect does not go through a pupal stage but emerges from the egg as a nymph that resembles the adult.

Midgut: The tube in an insect's abdomen where food is digested; with the foregut and hindgut it makes up the digestive system.

Molt: To shed the outer skin.

Nectar: A sugary liquid produced by flowers to attract insects; the chief raw ingredient of honey.

Nervous system: In insects, the system consisting of the brain, the nerve cord, ganglia, and sense receptors for hearing, seeing, and smelling. The **central nervous system** consists of the brain, the nerve cord, and ganglia.

Nymph: The immature, wingless stage just after hatching in insect species that undergo incomplete metamorphosis.

Ocellus: A light-sensitive organ that responds to changes in light intensity but cannot form images.

Olfactory: Having to do with the sense of smell.

Ommatidium: One of the elements that make up the compound eye of an arthropod.

Order: A category of biological classification between family and class; includes related families.

Osmeterium: A Y-shaped scent gland on the head of some caterpillars.

Ostium: One of a series of openings in the dorsal vessel through which blood flows to the organs; the plural is ostia.

Palp: A feeler attached to the lower mouthparts of an insect.

Parasite: An animal that lives in or on another animal, called a host. The presence of a parasite usually harms its host.

Pedicel: The second segment of the insect antenna, between the scape and the flagellum.

Pheromone: A chemical given off by certain animals that causes a response by members of that species.

Phylum: The most inclusive category of biological classification within a kingdom; includes related classes.

Pleural arch: The structure in a flea's hind leg that generates, stores, and releases energy needed for jumping.

Postmentum: The part of the lower jaw of the dragonfly nymph that is attached to the head.

Prementum: The part of the lower jaw of the dragonfly nymph that is attached to the postmentum.

Proboscis: In insects, an extended tubular mouthpart.

Pteridines: A class of pigments found in butterfly and moth wings.

Pupa: The nonfeeding, usually inactive stage between the larval stage and adult in insects that undergo complete metamorphosis.

Queen substance: A pheromone secreted by queen bees and consumed by worker bees that inhibits the building of queen cells and the development of worker-bee ovaries.

Resilin: A rubberlike protein from which the pleural arch of the flea is made.

Retractor muscle: A muscle that works with a protractor muscle to extend and withdraw a body part.

Rhabdom: A type of cell in the ommatidium that contains pigments that absorb light.

Royal jelly: A nutritious substance produced by worker honeybees and fed to larvae for a few days and to queen larvae for a longer period.

Rudimentary wings: Immature or incomplete wings.

Scape: The section of the antenna that attaches to the head.

Sensillum: A simple sense organ.

Silk: In spiders, a liquid protein produced by the silk gland that hardens as it leaves the spinnerets; used for making webs, wrapping prey, and producing egg sacs.

Social insect: A species of insects that live in organized communities.

Solitary insect: A species of insects that do not live in organized communities.

Species: The most specific category of biological classification. It includes organisms that can interbreed and produce fully functional offspring.

Spigot: In spiders, the structure at the end of the spinneret from which the silk is released.

Spinneret: The muscular structure on the rear end of a spider's abdomen that produces silk to build webs and wrap up prey.

Spiracles: Openings in the side of an insect through which air enters.

Stylet: In insects, a needlelike mouthpart.

Symbiosis: The close association between two different types of organisms to the benefit of one or both of them. In **mutualism,** both organisms benefit from the relationship.

Tarsus: One of the four main insect leg parts, along with the tibia, femur, and coxa.

Thorax: The midsection of an insect's body; it carries the legs and wings.

Tibia: The lower leg between the tarsus and femur; one of the four main parts of the insect leg along with the tarsus, femur, and coxa.

Trachea: In insects, a tube that delivers oxygen, taken in through the spiracles, to the tracheoles.

Tracheoles: Tiny tubes in an insect body that deliver oxygen to the cells and pick up carbon dioxide.

Trochanter: A small segment of the insect leg between the coxa and femur.

Tubuliformes gland: The gland in spiders that produces silk for making egg sacs.

Tympanic organ: A hearing organ in insects.

Ventral chain: The central nerve cord that runs the length of the body on the underside of an insect.

Weevil: A type of beetle with a snout that contains the mouthparts at the end.

Index

K

Staff for
UNDERSTANDING SCIENCE & NATURE

Editorial Director: Karin Kinney
Assistant Editor/Research: Elizabeth Thompson
Editorial Assistant: Louisa Potter
Production Manager: Prudence G. Harris
Senior Copy Coordinator: Juli Duncan
Production: Celia Beattie
Library: Louise D. Forstall
Computer Composition: Deborah G. Tait (Manager), Monika D.
    Thayer, Janet Barnes Syring, Lillian Daniels

Special Contributors, Text: Joe Alper, Marfé Ferguson Delano,
    Margery duMond, Stephen Hart, Gina Maranto, Mark Washburn
Research: Jocelyn Lindsay
Design/Illustration: Antonio Alcalá, Caroline Brock,
    Nicholas Fasciano, Al Kettler, David Neal Wiseman
Photography: Cover: Stephen Dalton/Animals Animals; 1: © Robert
    Noonan; 27: Robert Maier/Animals Animals; 63: Alastair Shay/
    Animals Animals; 82, 83: E. R. Degginger/Animals Animals; 117:
    Breck P. Kent/Animals Animals; 137: Agriculture Research
    Service, USDA
Index: Barbara L. Klein

Consultants:
Carol Sheppard and Steve Sheppard are entomologists with the
U.S. Department of Agriculture.

Library of Congress Cataloging-in-Publication Data
Insects & spiders.
        p.   cm. — (Understanding science & nature)
    Includes index.
    Summary: Questions and answers present information about
the physical characteristics, behavior, nests, and defenses of insects and spiders.
    ISBN 0-8094-9687-9 (trade) — ISBN 0-8094-9688-7 (lib. bdg.)
    1. Insects—Juvenile literature. 2. Spiders—Juvenile literature.
[1. Insects—Miscellanea. 2. Spiders—Miscellanea. 3. Questions
and answers.]
I. Time-Life Books.   II. Title: Insects and spiders.
III. Series.
QL467.2.I583   1993
595.7—dc20   92-30847
                                                        CIP
                                                        AC

TIME-LIFE for CHILDREN ®

Publisher: Robert H. Smith
Associate Publisher and Managing Editor: Neil Kagan
Assistant Managing Editor: Patricia Daniels
Editorial Directors: Jean Burke Crawford, Allan Fallow,
    Karin Kinney, Sara Mark, Elizabeth Ward
Director of Marketing: Margaret Mooney
Product Managers: Cassandra Ford, Shelley L. Schimkus
Director of Finance: Lisa Peterson
Financial Analyst: Patricia Vanderslice
Administrative Assistant: Barbara A. Jones
Special Contributor: Jacqueline A. Ball

Original English translation by International Editorial Services Inc./
C. E. Berry

First printing. Printed in U.S.A.
Published simultaneously in Canada.
Time Life Inc. is a wholly owned subsidiary of
THE TIME INC. BOOK COMPANY.
TIME-LIFE is a trademark of Time Warner Inc. U.S.A.
For subscription information, call 1-800-621-7026.